THE

Extreme

NEW TESTAMENT

BIBLE

TRIVIA

Challenge

TROY SCHMIDT

D0827302

BroadStreet
P U B L I S H I N G

BroadStreet Publishing Group, LLC
Racine, Wisconsin, USA
BroadStreetPublishing.com

The Extreme New Testament Bible Trivia Challenge

Copyright © 2016 by Troy Schmidt

ISBN-13: 978-1-4245-5239-9 (softcover)

ISBN-13: 978-1-4245-5271-9 (e-book)

Stock or custom editions of BroadStreet Publishing titles may be purchased in bulk for educational, business, ministry, fundraising, or sales promotional use. For information, please e-mail info@broadstreetpublishing.com.

Cover design by Chris Garborg at www.garborgdesign.com.
Typesetting by Katherine Lloyd at www.theDESKonline.com

Printed in the United States of America

16 17 18 19 20 5 4 3 2 1

Contents

PART 1: THE QUESTIONS • 5

PART 2: THE ANSWERS • 157

PART ONE

THE
QUESTIONS

★ THE ★
Extreme
NEW TESTAMENT
Challenge

Matthew

1. Matthew's genealogy of Jesus begins with what person? *Abraham*

2. Which of the twelve tribes did Jesus descend from? *Judah*

3. Name the five women mentioned in Jesus' genealogy from the Gospel of Matthew. *Tamar, Rehab, Ruth, Bathsheba, Mary*

4. Matthew's genealogy of Jesus included what woman who tricked her father-in-law into sleeping with her? *Tamar*

5. Who was the son of Boaz and Ruth in Matthew's genealogy of Jesus? *Obed*

6. Only one unnamed woman is mentioned in Matthew's genealogy as the "wife" of someone else. Who was it? *Bathsheba*

7. Who was the father of Joseph, the husband of Mary in Matthew's genealogy? ~~Joseph~~ *Jacob*

8. Three sets of how many generations are mentioned in Matthew's genealogy? *fourteen*

9. According to Matthew 1, how did Mary become pregnant? *Holy Spirit*

10. What did Joseph quietly want to do to Mary *put her away Divorce*

11. Who told Joseph to name the boy Jesus? *Angel*

12. Joseph was told to name the boy Jesus because he would save his people from what? *their sins*

13. What prophet did Matthew quote that said the virgin would give birth to a child? *Isaiah*

14. What name will people call Jesus because it means "God with us"? *Emmanuel*

15. In what town was Jesus born? *Bethlehem*

16. In what region was Bethlehem located at the time of Jesus? *Judea*

17. Who was king in Israel when Jesus was born? *Herod*

18. From what direction in relation to Jerusalem did the magi come? *East*

19. What sign did the magi see in the sky? *Star*

20. Besides King Herod, who else was disturbed by the news of a new king?

21. What two groups of scholars did Herod question about the Christ? *Priests + teachers*

22. What prophet did the scholars quote to indicate the coming king's birthplace? *Micah*

23. In what kind of structure did the magi find Mary and Jesus? *house*

24. What three gifts did the wise men give Jesus? *Gold frankincense + myrrh*

25. How were the wise men warned not to go back to Herod? *a dream*

26. How was Joseph told to go to Egypt? *a dream*

27. What prophet's book did Matthew quote to confirm the prophecy of Jesus going to Egypt? *Hosea*

28. Mary, Joseph and Jesus stayed in Egypt until what happened? *Herod died*

29. Herod killed the boys up to what age in Bethlehem? *2 yrs*

30. What Old Testament prophet did Matthew say predicted Herod's killing of Bethlehem's boys? *Jeremiah*

31. How many total dreams did Joseph have in the book of Matthew? *four*

32. What king caused Joseph to fear returning to Bethlehem and thus forced them to move to Galilee? *Archelaus*

33. Who was Archelaus' father? *Herod*

34. After Egypt, where did Joseph move his family when they returned to Israel? *nazareth*

35. In what district was Nazareth found? *Galilee*

36. By living in Nazareth, Jesus could now be called a what? *a Nazarene*

37. What Old Testament prophet did Matthew say predicted John the Baptist's desert calling? *Isaiah*

38. What were John the Baptist's clothes made of? *Camel hair*

39. What was John the Baptist's belt made of? *leather*

40. What two food items did John the Baptist eat? *locusts & honey*

41. In what river did John the Baptist baptize? *Jordan*

42. What two groups of religious leaders did John the Baptist verbally attack? *Pharasees + Sadducees*

43. John the Baptist said any tree that doesn't produce what must be cut down? *fruit*

44. What two things did John the Baptist say the coming one would baptize with? *Holy Ghost + fire*

45. Two times God spoke to people about Jesus and said, "This is my son." When were they? *Baptism + transfiguration*

46. What descended on Jesus like a dove at his baptism? *Holy Spirit*

47. How many days and nights did Jesus fast in the wilderness? *40*

48. What did satan want Jesus to turn the stones into during the temptation? *Bread*

49. Jesus responded to satan and said that man does not only live on bread but on what? *the Word of God*

50. During the temptations, satan took Jesus to the highest point of what structure? *temple*

51. What did satan tell Jesus to do from that building's highest point? *himself down*

52. Who did satan say would catch Jesus if he fell? *angels*

53. What book of the Bible did satan quote to Jesus during the temptation? *Psalms 91*

54. What book of the Bible did Jesus quote back to satan three times during the temptation? *Deut.*

55. After the temptation, who came and attended to Jesus? *angels*

56. In Matthew 4, Jesus left Nazareth and went to live in what city? *Capernaum*

57. When Jesus moved to this region, it fulfilled a prophecy by what Old Testament prophet? *Isaiah*

58. On what sea's coastline did Jesus meet Simon Peter? *Galilee*

59. Who was Peter's brother? *Andrew*

60. What was Peter's occupation? *fisherman*

61. What were the names of the two sons of Zebedee? *James + John*

62. What was the occupation of those sons of Zebedee? *fishermen*

63. What were they fixing when they saw Jesus? *nets*

64. What two things did Matthew 4 say the sons of Zebedee left to follow Jesus? *boat + father*

65. According to Matthew 4, news about Jesus spread as far as what other country? *Syria*

66. According to the Beatitudes, which kingdom do the poor in spirit inherit? *heaven*

67. According to the Beatitudes, who did Jesus promise will be comforted? *those who mourn*

68. According to the Beatitudes, what will the meek inherit? *earth*

69. According to the Beatitudes, God bless those who hunger and thirst after what? *righteousness*

70. According to the Beatitudes, which group will see God? *pure*

71. According to the Beatitudes, which group was called sons/children of God? *Peace makers*

72. What earthly seasoning did Jesus warn people not to lose or they would be good for nothing? *salt*

73. What did Jesus say people should never put under a bowl? *light*

74. As people let their light shine before others, what did Jesus want them to see? *Good deeds*

75. What two things did Jesus say he did not come to abolish? *Law*

76. Jesus told his followers that to enter the kingdom of heaven their righteousness must surpass whose? *Pharisees*

77. What Aramaic curse word did Jesus tell his followers not to call their brothers? *Raca*

78. What two body parts did Jesus say it was better to cut off than for the whole body to go to hell? *eye + hand*

79. Which hand—right or left—did Jesus say it was better to do without? *right*

80. What was the one reason for divorce cited by Jesus? *adultery*

81. What four things should a person not swear by? *moeh*

82. Which cheek—right or left—did Jesus mention being slapped before a person offers the other? *Left*

83. What article of clothing did Jesus say to give to someone if they sue you for your shirt/tunic? *coat*

84. What occupation did Jesus mention that loves those that love them? *tax collectors*

85. What did Jesus warn us not to practice before men?

86. When we give to the needy, we should not announce it with what musical instrument? *trumpets*

87. According to Jesus, in what two public places do hypocrites like to pray? *Street synagogue*

88. When teaching about prayer, Jesus told his followers not to babble like whom? *Pagans*

89. When we pray, what food should we ask God to give us daily? *bread*

90. What two makeup tips did Jesus give for fasting? *oil on head → wash face*

91. What insect did Jesus say destroys our treasures?

92. What part of the body did Jesus say was the lamp of the body? *eye*

93. Who are the two masters Jesus said we can't serve at the same time? *God & money*

94. What three things in nature did Jesus use as examples for not worrying?

95. What two things did Jesus say we must seek first before anything else? *birds & lilies*

96. What did Jesus tell us we should remove from our own eye before pointing out the speck of sawdust in someone else's eye? *plank*

97. What piece of jewelry did Jesus tell us not to toss to pigs, as a figure of speech? *pearls*

98. What did Jesus say a father will not give his son if the son asked for bread? *stone*

99. What did Jesus say a father would not give his son if the son asked for fish? *snake*

100. Jesus said a wide gate and broad road lead to what? *destruction*

101. Jesus said a small gate and a narrow road lead to what? *life*

102. What did Jesus say the false prophets appeared dressed in to fool people? *Sheep's clothing*

103. What ferocious animal did Jesus compare false prophets to? *wolves*

104. How did Jesus say you can recognize a false prophet? *By their fruit*

105. What three things do the religious do, but, on judgment day, Jesus said that he wouldn't know them? *prophecy Cast out demons Miracle*

106. On what material did Jesus say wise men build their house? *rock*

107. What three weather occurrences try to bring down the house built on rock? *rain flood wind*

108. The people said Jesus taught as one having what quality? *authority*

109. What was Jesus "willing" to cleanse a man of in Matthew 8? *leprosy*

110. Who did the Roman centurion want Jesus to heal? *His servant*

111. In Matthew 8, to whom did Jesus say, "I have not found anyone in Israel with such great faith"? *Centurion*

112. Which apostle's mother-in-law did Jesus heal? *Peters*

113. What kind of a sickness did she have? *fever*

114. What did Jesus touch that made her sickness go away? *Her hand*

115. What did she do after she was healed? *Got up + waited on them*

116. According to Jesus, what two animals have homes, but he, the Son of Man, had no place to lay his head? *foxes + birds*

117. What was Jesus doing in the boat when the storm struck? *sleeping*

118. In Matthew 8, how many demon-possessed men met Jesus in the region of Gadarenes? *two*

119. Where did those demon-possessed men live? *Cemetary*

120. Into what herd of animals did Jesus cast the demons? *pigs*

121. After Jesus healed the demon-possessed men, what did the town want Jesus to do? *Go away*

122. What did Jesus do first to the paralyzed man that caused the teachers to call Jesus a blasphemer? *Forgive him of sin*

123. What did Jesus tell the healed man to pick up and go home? *His mat* Bed

124. What was Matthew sitting in when Jesus called? *tax coll. booth*

125. What two groups of people did Matthew 9:10 say were eating with Jesus and the disciples? *tax collectors + sinners*

126. At whose house were they dining? *matt's house*

127. What did Jesus tell the Pharisees the sick need but not the healthy? *a doctor*

128. Jesus told the Pharisees he desired mercy but not what? *sacrifice*

129. Jesus told the Pharisees he did not come to call the righteous but the what? *sinners*

130. Jesus said people do not sew what kind of cloth on a garment? *unshrunk*

131. According to Jesus, what shouldn't people pour new wine into? *old wine skins*

132. What religious title did the father of the dead girl hold? *synagogue leader*

133. How many years had the woman been bleeding until Jesus healed her? *12 yrs*

134. What did the bleeding woman want to touch and knew she would be healed when she did? *Jesus's cloak*

135. What instrument were the mourners playing when Jesus entered the dead girl's house? *pipes*

136. Jesus told the mourners that the girl was not dead but what? *asleep*

137. What was the crowd's response when Jesus said the girl was not dead? *they laughed*

138. What prophetic title did the two blind men call Jesus? *Son of David*

139. What supernatural explanation caused the man to be mute? *Demonic*

140. According to Jesus, the harvest was plentiful but what were there few of? *workers*

141. When the apostles are listed, who is always put first? *Peter*

142. Which apostle was known as the Zealot? *Simon*

143. When the apostles are listed, who is always put last? *Judas Iscariot*

144. When Jesus sent out the twelve disciples, what towns did he say to avoid? *Samaritans*

145. Who did Jesus tell them to go to instead? *Lost sheep of Israel*

146. What items did Jesus tell the twelve not to take with them?

147. What did Jesus say to do to unfriendly towns as they left? *shake dust off feet*

148. Jesus said if a town rejected them, it would be more bearable for what twin city than for that town? *Sodom + Gomorrah*

149. What reptile did Jesus tell his followers to be as shrewd as? *snake*

150. What bird did Jesus tell his followers to be as innocent as? *dove*

151. Where did Jesus warn them that they would be flogged? *Synagogue*

152. Jesus said not to worry about what to say because who would be speaking through them? *Holy Spirit*

153. Jesus said not to worry about the one who could kill the body, but to fear the one who could kill what? *The soul*

154. According to Jesus, how many sparrows are sold for a penny? *two*

155. What part of our body did Jesus say God has numbered? *hairs on our head*

156. Jesus said he did not come to bring peace, but what? *a sword*

157. What four family members did Jesus say we could not love more than him? *Father mother son daughter*

158. What did Jesus tell followers to take up and follow him? *their cross*

159. Jesus said someone will not lose their reward if they give what to one of those little ones? *a cup of water*

160. Jesus asked the people if they went out into the desert to see what being swayed by the wind? *a reed*

161. In Matthew 11, what did Jesus say that they saw in the wilderness? *a prophet*

162. What Old Testament book did Jesus quote as prophetic proof about John the Baptist?

163. Who did Jesus say was the Elijah to come?

164. Because Jesus feasted and drank, what did he say people called him?

165. What two cities did Jesus say were worse than Tyre and Sidon?

166. What city did Jesus say was worse off than Sodom because it rejected Jesus' miracles?

167. In Matthew 11, Jesus praised his Father for hiding things from the wise and revealing them to who?

168. What farming tool did Jesus ask us to take of his and learn from?

169. What part of us did Jesus promise to find rest for?

170. What did Jesus' disciples pick and eat on the Sabbath?

171. Jesus compared his disciples' actions on the Sabbath to the men of what king who ate the consecrated bread of the temple?

172. What animals did Jesus ask the priests if they would pull out of a pit on the Sabbath?

173. What withered part of the man did Jesus heal on the Sabbath and anger the Pharisees?

174. According to Isaiah and quoted in Matthew, what bruised object will the chosen one not break?

175. And what smoldering object will he not snuff out?

176. From where did the Pharisees think Jesus got his power?

177. Jesus said blasphemy against who would not be forgiven?

178. In Matthew 12, what did Jesus say every man will have to give an account for on the day of judgment?

179. In Matthew 12, what kind of a generation would seek after a sign, according to Jesus?

180. Jesus compared his (upcoming) three days in the heart of the earth to what Old Testament prophet's three-day adventure?

181. When a spirit leaves a person then returns and finds it empty and swept clean, how many more spirits will it invite to move in?

182. In Jesus' parable of the soils, what creature ate up the seed scattered on the path?

183. What does the seed represent in the parable of the soils?

184. What do the thorns represent in the parable of the soils?

185. How many more times blessed are those who accept God's message in the parable of the soils?

186. In a parable, what did Jesus say the enemy planted in a field of wheat?

187. What seed did Jesus call the smallest of all the seeds?

188. In a parable using bread, what did the woman use that permeated the dough?

189. In the parable of the weeds, what did the field represent?

190. In the parable of the weeds, what did the good seed represent?

191. In the parable of the weeds, who did the enemy represent?

192. Who were the harvesters in Jesus' parable of the weeds?

193. In a parable Jesus spoke, what did the man find in a field that caused him to sell everything and buy it?

194. Name four of Jesus' siblings mentioned in Matthew 13.

195. Who did Jesus say has no honor in his hometown?

196. Because of his hometown's lack of faith, what did he do few of while there?

197. What was the full title of the Herod who had John the Baptist killed?

198. Who was Herod's wife?

199. When Herod took Philip's wife, what was Philip's relationship to Herod?

200. Whose daughter danced for Herod?

201. What was the occasion that she danced at?

202. Who did Herod have beheaded?

203. Where was John already when they came to behead him?

204. What was his head displayed on?

205. Who buried John the Baptist's body?

206. At the feeding of the 5,000, how much fish and bread did the disciples find?

207. How many baskets of broken pieces were left over?

208. Around what time of the day did Jesus walk out on water and meet his disciples?

209. When they saw Jesus on the water, what did the disciples think he was?

210. Who asked to join Jesus on the water?

211. What did Peter see that frightened him and caused him to sink?

212. In Matthew 14, what was the only thing of Jesus' the people wanted to touch, believing it would heal them (and it did)?

213. Who did the disciples believe that Jesus had offended when talking about hand washing?

214. Where do blind guides lead the blind, according to Jesus?

215. What was the Canaanite woman's daughter suffering from?

216. Jesus told the Canaanite woman that it was not right to take the children's bread and toss it to what?

217. What did the Canaanite woman say the dogs would eat when it fell off the table?

218. How many days were the people with Jesus without food before he decided to feed the 4,000?

219. How many loaves of bread did Jesus start with to feed the 4,000?

220. How many basketfuls of bread were left over at the feeding of the 4,000?

221. Jesus told the Pharisees that they understood how to interpret the sky when was what color?

222. When talking about yeast and bread, Jesus was guarding the people against the teachings of what two groups?

223. When Jesus said, "Who do people say that I am," which three prophets did the apostles name?

224. What substance did Jesus tell Peter he would build his church on?

225. Jesus said the gates of what would not overcome his church?

226. Who did Jesus tell to get behind him when talking to Peter?

227. Which three apostles were invited up to the mountain where the transfiguration occurred?

228. When Jesus transfigured, what did his face shine like?

229. What two Old Testament people appeared on the mountain with Jesus?

230. What did Peter offer to build for the occasion?

231. In reference to Elijah coming some day soon, who did the disciples understand Elijah was?

232. What two things did the boy suffering from seizures throw himself into?

233. According to Jesus, why couldn't the disciples cast out demons?

234. What tax did the collectors question if Jesus was going to pay?

235. How much was that tax?

236. What was the value of the coin, in drachmas, that Jesus said they would find in the mouth of the fish?

237. According to Jesus in Matthew 18, what should people humble themselves like to enter the kingdom of God?

238. If someone caused a little one to stumble in his faith, what should a millstone be tied around before they were thrown into the sea?

239. What three body parts did Jesus say it was better to live without than to live with and sin?

240. How many total sheep did the man in the parable have before one wandered away?

241. If something is bound or loosed on earth, where else will it be bound and loosed?

242. God will agree in heaven if a minimum of how many people ask and agree on earth?

243. How many times did Peter ask if people should be forgiven?

244. According to Matthew 18, how many times did Jesus say a person should be forgiven?

245. In the parable of the unmerciful servant, how much did the servant owe his master?

246. Over how much money did the servant choke another servant?

247. According to Jesus, why did Moses permit divorce?

248. According to Jesus, what was the only reason for divorce?

249. Who did Jesus tell the rich young man to give his money to?

250. According to Jesus in Matthew 19, it's hard for whom to enter the kingdom of God?

251. Jesus said it's easier for a camel to go through what than for the rich to get into heaven?

252. Who did Jesus say his followers would sit on thrones and judge?

253. Jesus said those who had left behind family and homes would receive a blessing of how many times more?

254. In the parable of the vineyard workers, how much was each worker paid no matter when they started to work?

255. The mother of whose sons asked Jesus if her boys could sit at his right and left in the kingdom?

256. In Matthew 20, for someone to be first, they must become what?

257. What did Jesus say the Son of Man gave as a ransom for many?

258. Before the triumphal entry, what two animals did Jesus ask his disciples to find?

259. What Old Testament prophet said Jesus would ride those two animals?

260. When Jesus entered Jerusalem for the triumphal entry, what two things did the people lay in the streets?

261. What does the word *Hosanna* mean?

262. In Matthew 21, Jesus tipped over the table of people selling what animal?

263. Jesus told the money changers that they were making his "house" a den of what?

264. What kind of tree did Jesus wither?

265. Jesus rebuked the Pharisees by asking if baptism was from heaven or from man?

266. What two groups of people did Jesus tell the Pharisees were getting into heaven before them?

267. In the parable of the tenants, who did the landowner send to collect the fruit after three sets of servants were killed?

268. In the parable of the tenants, what did the tenants do to the son?

269. According to Jesus, what did the stone become that the builders rejected?

270. In the parable of the wedding banquet, who was throwing a banquet?

271. In the parable of the wedding banquet, what was the occasion that inspired the banquet?

272. In the parable of the wedding banquet, what did the invited people do to the servants who were inviting them to the banquet?

273. Where did the servants eventually go to invite people to the banquet?

274. In the parable of the wedding banquet, what was the guest not wearing that caused him to get thrown out?

275. Where did they throw the man not wearing the wedding clothes?

276. What was the value of the coin used for the tax that Jesus asked to see?

277. Whose portrait was on the coin that Jesus asked to see?

278. What opposition group quizzed Jesus on marriage at the resurrection?

279. How many brothers were in the marriage/resurrection question Jesus was asked?

280. Jesus said that at the resurrection people do not marry similar to what unmarried group?

281. Who asked Jesus which was the greatest commandment in the law?

282. Whose son did the Pharisees agree the Messiah would be?

283. Jesus said the Pharisees wouldn't lift one thing to help people. What was it?

284. What did the Pharisees wear wide on their clothing?

285. What did the Pharisees like to be called in the marketplace?

286. In Matthew 23, how many "woes" did Jesus pronounce on the Pharisees?

287. When the Pharisees made a convert, according to Jesus, he became twice the son of what place?

288. Which three spices did Jesus say Pharisees gave a tenth of?

289. Jesus said the Pharisees strained out a gnat but swallowed a what?

290. Jesus said the Pharisees kept what two pieces of kitchenware clean but not themselves?

291. Jesus said Pharisees were like whitewashed what?

292. What reptiles did Jesus compare Pharisees to?

293. The blood of what two martyrs did Jesus reference in Matthew 23?

294. Jesus said he longed to gather the children of Jerusalem together like what farm animals?

295. What building did Jesus predict would be destroyed?

296. On what mountain did Jesus proclaim his Olivet Discourse?

297. What did Jesus warn his followers that they would hear rumors of?

298. Because of wickedness, what did Jesus say would grow cold?

299. In Matthew 24, Jesus predicted those abominable days would be dreadful for what two groups of women?

300. What two groups of people will speak during those dark days and declare false things?

301. According to Matthew 24, in those last days, what two celestial bodies will go dark?

302. Jesus said heaven and earth will pass away, but what will never pass away?

303. Jesus said no one would know when that day will arrive except whom?

304. Jesus said that day of judgment could be compared to the days of whom?

305. Where were the two men standing when one was taken and the other was left?

306. What were the two women grinding with when one was taken and the other was left?

307. In the parable, how many virgins took their lamps to go out and meet the bridegroom?

308. How many virgins were foolish and how many wise?

309. What did the foolish virgins forget to take with them?

310. At what time did the bridegroom show up?

311. In the parable of the talents, the man gave each servant talents based on what?

312. What did the person with one talent do with his money?

313. The master complimented the servants by saying, "Well done, _____ and _____ servant."

314. What kind of a man did the servant with one talent think his master was?

315. Where was this worthless servant thrown?

316. In Matthew 25, Jesus described a separation of believers and non-believers as the separation of what two flocks of animals?

317. What five conditions did Jesus reference by saying if you helped someone like this you helped him?

318. Jesus was crucified during what Jewish holiday?

319. In whose palace did the chief priests and elders meet to plot to kill Jesus?

320. In Matthew 26, Jesus was anointed with the alabaster jar of perfume while in whose home?

321. Instead of anointing Jesus with the perfume, where did the disciples think this money could have been better spent?

322. How many pieces of silver did Judas accept to betray Jesus?

323. Jesus predicted that one who had dipped his hand into what would betray him?

324. Which two apostles did Jesus predict would betray and deny him?

325. After they ate the Last Supper, Jesus and the apostles sang a hymn and then went to what mount?

326. What was the name of the garden where Jesus was arrested?

327. Before his arrest, what did Jesus pray for his father to take away from him?

328. How many times did the disciples fall asleep in the garden before Jesus' arrest?

329. What weapons did the mob bring with them to arrest Jesus?

330. What signal did Judas arrange with the captors to indicate which person was Jesus?

331. What part of the servant's body was cut off by a companion of Jesus?

332. How many legions of angels did Jesus say he could call down in the garden of Gethsemane?

333. Name the high priest Jesus saw first after being arrested.

334. Two false witnesses provided testimony saying Jesus told others he was going to destroy what, then rebuild it in three days?

335. During Jesus' arrest, who recognized Peter in the courtyard the first time?

336. During Jesus' arrest, who recognized Peter in the gateway the second time?

337. Which of Peter's traits gave him away as a friend of Jesus during Jesus' arrest?

338. Because of the accusations about his relationship with Jesus, what did Peter call down as he swore at his accusers?

339. How many times did Peter deny Christ?

340. What animal crowed to indicate Peter's denial?

341. What did Judas do with the thirty silver coins when the priests refused to take them back?

342. How did Judas kill himself?

343. What was the name of the field bought with the money Judas received to betray Jesus?

344. The book of Matthew says that the purchase of the potter's field with Judas' betrayal money fulfilled a prophecy written by which prophet?

345. Who was the Roman governor that Jesus faced on trial?

346. Who was the prisoner that the people wanted released instead of Jesus?

347. Who in Pilate's family had a bad dream because of Jesus?

348. When Pilate asked the crowd what to do with Jesus, what was the crowd's response?

349. What did Pilate do with the bowl of water before all the people?

350. What color robe did the guards put on Jesus before the crucifixion?

351. Where was the man from who carried Jesus' cross?

352. What was the name of the place where Jesus was crucified?

353. What does the name mean?

354. What did the guards offer Jesus to drink?

355. What crimes did the two men on both sides of Jesus commit?

356. From what book of the Bible did Jesus quote, "My God, my God, why have you forsaken me?"

357. Which Old Testament prophet did eyewitnesses think Jesus was calling out to from the cross?

358. When Jesus died, what tore in two?

359. Who, during the crucifixion, said, "Surely this is the Son of God"?

360. According to Matthew 27, name the women who witnessed the crucifixion.

361. From what town was Joseph, the rich man who gave Jesus his tomb?

362. What kind of material was the cloth made of that they wrapped Jesus' body in?

363. What two things did Pilate do to the tomb of Jesus so the disciples would not steal Jesus' body?

364. According to Matthew, the angel's appearance at the tomb was described as what weather occurrence?

365. According to Matthew, the angel's clothes at the tomb were described as what weather condition?

366. Where did the angel and Jesus tell his followers to go meet him after the resurrection?

367. What did the religious leaders tell everyone to explain the disappearance of Jesus' body?

368. In what region was the mountain located that Jesus gave the Great Commission in Matthew 28?

369. What four things did Jesus tell his followers to do at the end of Matthew 28?

370. What Old Testament prophet did Mark quote in reference to John the Baptist?

371. Mark 1:4 says John the Baptist was preaching a certain kind of baptism. What was it?

372. In what river did John the Baptist baptize?

373. John the Baptist's clothes were made from the hair of what animal?

374. What did John the Baptist wear around his waist?

375. What two things did John the Baptist eat?

376. John the Baptist said he was unworthy to tie what part of the sandal of the one coming after him?

377. John the Baptist said he baptized with water, but what did he say the one who was coming would baptize with?

378. During Jesus' baptism, what descended on him like a dove?

379. Mark 1 says that Jesus was with two groups in the desert after the temptation. What were they?

380. What were the occupations of Simon, Andrew, James, and John?

381. What did Simon and Andrew drop to follow Jesus?

382. Who was James and John's father?

383. In Mark 1, who did Jesus tell to be quiet in the Capernaum synagogue?

384. Whose mother-in-law did Jesus heal?

385. What was she suffering from?

386. What did Peter's mother-in-law do after she was healed?

387. What did Jesus command the demons not to reveal?

388. What was the man suffering from that Jesus was willing to cleanse him of?

389. Who did Jesus tell the now-cleansed leper to go show himself to?

390. In what city did the men lower their paralytic friend through the roof?

391. What did Jesus do before healing the paralytic?

392. Two apostles, James and Levi, have a father by the same name. What is it?

393. What two groups of people dined with Jesus at Matthew's house that angered the Pharisees?

394. Jesus said, "It is not the healthy who need a doctor" but who?

395. What practice did John's disciples do that the Pharisees pointed out Jesus' disciples didn't do?

396. What did Jesus say no one poured new wine into?

397. When Jesus' disciples picked the heads of grain, the Pharisees accused them of breaking which rule?

398. In Mark 3, what illness was the man in the synagogue afflicted with that Jesus healed him of on the Sabbath, causing the Pharisees to plot Jesus' death?

399. In Mark 3, who did the Pharisees conspire with to kill Jesus?

400. Jesus gave James and John the name *Boanerges*, which means what?

401. Who did the teachers of the law accuse Jesus of conspiring with to drive out demons?

402. What three things did Jesus say cannot be divided against themselves and stand?

403. Jesus said that whoever blasphemes against whom will not be forgiven?

404. Jesus said that his true mother and brothers were those who do what?

405. Name the four types of soils from Jesus' parable.

406. What animal ate up the first seed in the parable?

407. How many times more did the crop of good seed multiply in the parable?

408. Jesus frequently told listeners that people with ears must do what?

409. What did Jesus say the seed represented in the parable of the soils?

410. Who did the birds that came and took the seed away represent in the parable?

411. What two things caused people to receive the word with joy but later the desire fell away?

412. What three things caused the word to be choked, making it unfruitful?

413. When Jesus talked about a lamp, he said people shouldn't put it under a bowl but where?

414. What type of seed did Jesus say was very small but grew very large?

415. What was Jesus sleeping on during the storm at sea?

416. In Mark 4, during the storm, what two specific things obeyed Jesus, surprising the disciples?

417. In what region did Jesus meet the demon-possessed man who lived in the tombs?

418. Where did the demon-possessed man live in Mark 5?

419. What could not detain the demon-possessed man because of his strength?

420. What was the demon's name who plagued the man who lived in the tombs?

421. Why did he have this name?

422. About how many pigs rushed into the lake when Jesus sent the demons into them?

423. What did the people of the town ask Jesus to do after they heard about the demon/pig event?

424. Where did the formerly demon-possessed man go to tell others how much Jesus had done for him?

425. In Mark 5, who was the man that pleaded for Jesus to heal his daughter?

426. What title did he hold?

427. How many years had the woman suffered with her bleeding?

428. The bleeding woman received healing by touching what?

429. What three apostles were allowed to witness Jesus bring Jairus' daughter back from the dead?

430. What phrase did Jesus say to Jairus' daughter that made her get up?

431. How old was Jairus' daughter at the time?

432. What was Jesus' occupation according to the crowd in Mark 6?

433. Name Jesus' brothers mentioned in Mark 6.

434. In addition to his mother and brothers, what other members of Jesus' family did the crowd know about?

435. Jesus said a prophet was without honor in what place?

436. What amazed Jesus about his hometown?

437. What did Jesus say the disciples should shake off their feet if a town rejected them?

438. Who did people believe Jesus was? Name three.

439. John the Baptist spoke out against Herod's relationship with whom?

440. To whom was Herodias previously married?

441. What was the name of Herod's brother?

442. What was Herod celebrating when Herodias' daughter danced for him?

443. What was the most that Herod was willing to give Herodias' daughter?

444. What did Herodias' daughter ask for?

445. What was John's head delivered on?

446. Who came and took John's body to bury it?

447. Before the feeding of the 5,000, Jesus had compassion on the crowd because they were like sheep without what?

448. How much money did the disciples calculate it would cost to feed the 5,000?

449. How many loaves did the disciples find before the feeding of the 5,000?

450. How many fish did the disciples collect before the feeding of the 5,000?

451. Jesus directed the people to sit in groups of what?

452. How many baskets were left over at the feeding of the 5,000?

453. What gender was counted in the 5,000?

454. During what time of the day did Jesus walk across the water to the disciples in the boat?

455. What did the men believe Jesus really was when they saw him walking on the water?

456. In Mark 7, when Jesus called the Pharisees hypocrites, he blasted them by quoting what Old Testament prophet?

457. What word did Jesus use that means a gift devoted to God?

458. Where was the woman from who spoke to Jesus about crumbs and dogs?

459. Who did the Syrophoenician woman want Jesus to drive the demons out of?

460. What two places on the deaf man did Jesus put his fingers to help him hear?

461. Jesus opened a man's ears by uttering what Aramaic word?

462. What did that Aramaic word mean?

463. How many days had the crowds been with Jesus before the feeding of the 4,000?

464. How many loaves did the apostles bring Jesus before the feeding of the 4,000?

465. How many fish did the apostles bring Jesus before the feeding of the 4,000?

466. How many basketfuls of bread pieces did they pick up after the feeding of the 4,000?

467. Jesus warned his disciples against the yeast of what two people?

468. How did Jesus heal the blind man's eyes at Bethsaida?

469. As the blind man's eyes opened in Mark 8, what did the people look like to him?

470. Where was Jesus when he asked the disciples who people said he was?

471. What three answers did the disciples give?

472. Which disciple took Jesus aside and rebuked him?

473. Who did Jesus tell to get behind him?

474. What did Jesus say satan was more concerned about than godly things?

475. Jesus warned his followers not to gain the whole world or they would lose what?

476. What three apostles joined Jesus on the Mount of Transfiguration?

477. On the Mount of Transfiguration, what dazzling color did Jesus' clothes appear to be?

478. Which two Old Testament men appeared with Jesus during the transfiguration?

479. Who offered to build shelters for all three of them?

480. Who did Jesus say, as the teachers of the law knew, must come back first?

481. Jesus healed a boy with an evil spirit that routinely threw him into what two elements?

482. What did the boy's father ask Jesus to help him overcome?

483. When it came to demon possession, Jesus said this kind of thing could only come out because of what?

484. Who did Jesus take into his arms and say whoever welcomes one of these, welcomes him?

485. Jesus said a man cannot lose his reward by simply giving someone what?

486. According to Jesus, if you caused a little one to stumble, what would be the best thing to tie around your neck?

487. What three body parts does Jesus say it is better to live without than to continue to sin throughout life?

488. Who did Jesus say wrote the law allowing divorce?

489. Who rebuked the people for bringing children to Jesus?

490. Jesus took the children into his arms, placed his hands on them, and did what?

491. What did the rich man say he had kept since he was a boy?

492. Jesus told the rich young man to sell everything so he could have treasure where?

493. Jesus said it was easier for a camel to go through the eye of a needle than for whom to enter heaven?

494. What two places did Jesus tell his disciples they must leave to follow God?

495. Jesus said those who left families and fields for him would receive how much more in the present age?

496. In Mark 10, what four physical attacks did Jesus prophesy would happen to him when handed over to the Gentiles?

497. Which two apostles asked to sit with Jesus when he came into his glory?

498. Where did the two sons of Zebedee want to sit when Jesus entered his glory?

499. What was the name of the blind man in Mark 10?

500. What did his name mean?

501. What did Jesus say healed the blind man?

502. What made the colt unique that Jesus wanted to ride into Jerusalem?

503. When Jesus entered Jerusalem for the triumphal entry, what two items did people spread out on the road?

504. After Jesus rode into Jerusalem, he retreated to what town?

505. In Mark 11, why were there no figs on the tree before Jesus withered it?

506. What did Jesus prevent people from doing through the temple courts after he overturned the tables?

507. What kind of den did Jesus accuse the people of turning the temple into?

508. What land mass did Jesus say those with faith could command to take a flying leap into the sea?

509. What question did Jesus ask the Pharisees instead of answering their question about his authority?

510. In the parable of the tenants, how many servants did the farmers kill?

511. Who was the last person that the vineyard owner sent to the tenants to collect rent, but they killed him too?

512. In Jesus' quote of Psalm 118, what has the rejected stone become?

513. What value of coin did Jesus ask to see when questioned about paying taxes?

514. Whose image was on that coin?

515. The Sadducees didn't believe what happened after people died?

516. The Sadducees tried to trick Jesus about divorce by telling a story about a widow and how many brothers?

517. What celestial being did not get married according to Jesus?

518. Jesus quoted what two Old Testament books in referencing the two greatest commandments?

519. How many coins did the widow put in the offering according to Mark 12?

520. What were the coins made of?

521. In Mark 13, Jesus sat on what mount and spoke about the signs of the end of the age?

522. Jesus predicted his disciples would be handed over to local councils and what would happen to them in the synagogues?

523. Jesus told the disciples not to worry about what to say when arrested because who would be speaking through them?

524. What two kinds of women will have the hardest time in those abominable days?

525. During what season did Jesus hope the devastation wouldn't occur?

526. On what did Jesus say the Son of Man was coming?

527. What kind of tree did Jesus say they could learn a lesson from?

528. Jesus said heaven and earth will pass away, but what won't?

529. In whose home was Jesus reclining when the woman with the perfume jar anointed him?

530. What was the perfume jar made of that the woman used to anoint Jesus with in Bethany?

531. What was the perfume made of that the woman used to anoint Jesus with in Bethany?

532. Who did people think the proceeds from this expensive perfume should have been given to?

533. What was the man carrying who would help them find a room for Passover?

534. During the Last Supper, what would the betrayer dip into a bowl with Jesus?

535. During the Last Supper, Jesus said the bread represented what?

536. During the Last Supper, Jesus said the wine represented what?

537. After the Passover meal, but before they climbed the Mount of Olives, what did Jesus and the apostles do?

538. Name the garden where Jesus asked that the cup be taken away from him.

539. Jesus predicted that what would crow before Peter disowned him three times?

540. How many times did Jesus find Peter and the others sleeping?

541. What two weapons were the crowd armed with when they came to arrest Jesus?

542. What signal did the betrayer give to indicate who Jesus was?

543. What was the occupation of the person whose ear was cut off?

544. What was the man in the garden of Gethsemane wearing before he was seized and ran off naked?

545. Since the chief priests could not find any evidence against Jesus, what needed to happen to convict him?

546. Who accused Peter twice of knowing Jesus?

547. Where did those by the fire believe Peter was from?

548. How many times did the rooster crow before Peter disowned Jesus three times?

549. Who was the prisoner released from custody instead of Jesus?

550. What crimes had he committed?

551. What did Pilate believe caused the chief priests to hand Jesus over to him?

552. Who stirred up the crowds to have Barabbas released?

553. What was the name of the palace where the soldiers took Jesus and beat him?

554. What color robe did the guards put on Jesus?

555. From what city did Jesus' cross-carrying assistant come?

556. What was that man's name?

557. The man who helped Jesus carry his cross had two sons. What were their names?

558. What does the word *Golgotha* mean?

559. Jesus was offered wine on the cross mixed with what?

560. At what time did they begin to crucify Jesus?

561. What did Jesus' offense read on the sign over his head?

562. What were the crimes committed by the men crucified on Jesus' right and left?

563. What did people hurl at Jesus as they passed by him on the cross?

564. At what hour did darkness come over the land?

565. At what hour did Jesus cry out, "My God, my God, why have you forsaken me?"

566. Who did the witnesses believe Jesus was calling out to on the cross?

567. Who saw how Jesus died and said, "Surely this is the Son of God"?

568. Name the three women the gospel of Mark said were present for Jesus' crucifixion.

569. Who asked to bury Jesus' body?

570. What was he a prominent member of?

571. Who released Jesus' body to him?

572. What kind of cloth was Jesus' body wrapped in?

573. Which two women in Mark 15 saw where Jesus had been laid?

574. What did the women bring to the tomb to anoint Jesus' body with?

575. What did the women worry was blocking the tomb?

576. Who announced to the women, "He is risen"?

577. Where did the angel say Jesus was going ahead of them?

578. How many demons does Mark 16 say Jesus drove out of Mary Magdalene?

579. How did Luke describe his information gathering to write this gospel?

580. Who did Luke write his Gospel to?

581. Who was John the Baptist's father?

582. What was his job?

583. Who was Zechariah's wife?

584. From whose genealogical line did both Zechariah and Elizabeth descend?

585. What was Zechariah chosen by lot to do inside the temple?

586. What name did the angel tell Zechariah and Elizabeth to give their son?

587. What did the angel say in Luke 1 that the priest's son should never drink?

588. The angel said John would go before the Lord in the spirit and power of what Old Testament prophet?

589. The angel quoted what Old Testament prophet to confirm John the Baptist's fulfillment of Scripture?

590. What was the angel's name?

591. What affliction struck Zechariah because he did not believe the angel?

592. In what town did Mary the mother of Jesus live?

593. Who was Mary pledged to be married to?

594. Whose throne would Jesus be given, according to Luke 1?

595. Over whose descendants did the angel say Mary's son would ruler?

596. Why was Mary skeptical that a baby could be born to her?

597. Who did the angel say would allow her to be pregnant?

598. Whose baby leapt in the womb when it came in contact with Mary?

599. How long did Mary stay with Elizabeth during her visit?

600. What did the people think Zechariah and Elizabeth's son should be named?

601. What name did Zechariah write on the writing table?

602. As soon as Zechariah wrote down that name, what happened to him?

603. Which two people both are credited with songs in Luke 1?

604. Where did John live before he appeared publicly to Israel?

605. Which Caesar was in charge of the census when Jesus was born?

606. Who was governor of Syria when the census was last taken?

607. To what town did Joseph travel to register for the census?

608. Joseph was from the house and line of whom?

609. When Jesus was born, what did Mary wrap him in?

610. When Jesus was born, what was used as his crib/bed?

611. After Jesus was born, who first heard about the news in Luke 2?

612. How many angels first showed up to tell them?

613. What sign did the angel tell the shepherds to look for?

614. After this message, how many angels showed up to the shepherds?

615. Where did Mary treasure up all these events and ponder them?

616. How many days after his birth was Jesus circumcised?

617. How many days after his birth was Jesus officially named?

618. Why did Mary, Joseph, and Jesus go to the temple in Luke 2 right after Jesus was born?

619. What pair of sacrifices did Joseph need to offer then?

620. Two people in the temple wanted to see the baby Jesus. Who were they?

621. What did Simeon say he needed to do before he died?

622. Who revealed that to Simeon?

623. Who was the female prophet that met Joseph, Mary, and Jesus in the temple?

624. After how many years of marriage did Anna's husband die?

625. After performing all the necessary purification rites, what town did Mary, Joseph, and Jesus return to?

626. After what celebration did Mary and Joseph lose track of Jesus?

627. How old was Jesus at this time?

628. After how many days traveling did Mary and Joseph realize Jesus was not with them?

629. After arriving in Jerusalem, how many days did it take Joseph and Mary to find Jesus?

630. Where did they find him?

631. When they found Jesus in Luke 2, who was he talking to?

632. What was the reaction of those who were talking to twelve-year-old Jesus?

633. Where did twelve-year-old Jesus tell his parents he could obviously be found?

634. Which Caesar was in charge when John the Baptist started his ministry?

635. Who was the governor of Judea when John the Baptist started his ministry?

636. Who was the tetrarch of Galilee when John the Baptist started his ministry?

637. Who were the two high priests in charge when John the Baptist started his ministry?

638. According to Luke, which Old Testament prophet's words did John's arrival in the desert fulfill?

639. From what did John the Baptist say God could raise up children of Israel?

640. What two occupations of people did Luke point out came to John the Baptist for baptism?

641. Who did John tell not to exhort money or accuse people falsely?

642. What article of the Messiah's clothing did John the Baptist say he was unworthy to untie?

643. What two things did John the Baptist say the Messiah would baptize with?

644. Herod threw John the Baptist in jail because John rebuked Herod's relationship with whom?

645. When Jesus was baptized, what was the Holy Spirit described as when he descended?

646. About how old was Jesus when he began his ministry?

647. The genealogy of Jesus in Luke begins with what person?

648. Who is the last person of Luke's genealogy of Jesus?

649. How many total days was Jesus fasting in the desert?

650. Which book of the Bible does Jesus quote back to the devil three times during the desert temptations?

651. What food did the devil tell Jesus to turn the stones into?

652. What did the devil show Jesus at the top of the high mountain place?

653. To the top of what structure in Jerusalem did the devil take Jesus?

654. What prophet did Jesus read from in the synagogue of his hometown in Nazareth?

655. After Jesus spoke in the synagogue in Nazareth, what did the people want to throw him off of?

656. What illness was Peter's mother-in-law suffering from?

657. What did Luke 4 say the demons shouted as Jesus cast them out of people?

658. What other name does the Lake of Gennesaret go by?

659. What were the fishermen doing to their nets when Jesus saw them?

660. As a result of the huge catch of fish, what began to happen to the boats?

661. Who fell to his knees as a result of this fishing miracle?

662. Who were Simon's fishing business partners?

663. What did Jesus tell them they would now fish for?

664. What disease did the man have that Jesus told him to go present himself to the priests after healing him?

665. What did the friends need to remove from the roof before lowering their friend through?

666. Before healing the paralytic man lowered through the roof, what did Jesus do when he saw their faith?

667. What was Levi sitting in when Jesus called him to follow?

668. What two groups of people did the Pharisees accuse Jesus of eating with at Levi's house?

669. What did Jesus say the sick needed, but not the healthy?

670. According to Jesus' metaphor, what do people not pour new wine into?

671. What work did Jesus' disciples do in the field on the Sabbath that the Pharisees called unlawful?

672. In Luke 6, who did Jesus heal on the Sabbath that the Pharisees were furious over?

673. Which three names do more than one apostle share?

674. If someone takes your cloak, what else did Jesus say to give them?

675. Who did Jesus say "loves those that love them"?

676. Jesus said a good measure pressed down, shaken together, and running over will be poured on your what?

677. Jesus said a blind man cannot lead a blind man because he will lead them both into a what?

678. Jesus said we shouldn't pay attention to the sawdust in our brother's eye because what it is in our eye?

679. According to Jesus in Luke 6, what doesn't a good tree produce?

680. A man speaks, Jesus said, out of the overflow of his what?

681. In Jesus' parable, a wise man built his house on what?

682. What was the occupation of the man who asked Jesus to heal his servant?

683. In Luke 7, the man told Jesus there was no need for him to come to his house to heal his servant, because all Jesus needed to do was what?

684. Jesus raised a widow's son from the dead. What town was this in?

685. What did Jesus touch to make the widow's son rise from the dead?

686. Whose disciples came to Jesus to verify he was the one they were all waiting for?

687. What two things did Jesus ask if people went out to the desert to see?

688. What prophet did Jesus quote to verify that John the Baptist fulfilled his prophecy?

689. Who did Jesus say that among those born of women there was no one greater?

690. In Luke 7:34, what "names" did the Pharisees call Jesus?

691. At whose house was Jesus when the woman anointed his feet?

692. What was the jar made of that the woman brought?

693. What was in the jar?

694. What did the woman with the jar keep kissing while she anointed Jesus?

695. Luke 8 mentions three followers who were women healed of demons and diseases. Who were they?

696. How many demons did Jesus release from Mary Magdalene?

697. One of the women Jesus healed of demons was the wife of a manager of whose household?

698. When the farmer from the parable of the sower spread the seed on the path, what came and ate it up?

699. According to the parable of the soils, why did the plants whither on the rock?

700. According to the parable of the soils, what choked the plants?

701. On the good soil, how many times more did the seed yield a crop than what was sown other places?

702. When Jesus explained the miracle, what was the seed?

703. According to the parable of the soils, who comes and takes away the word from people's hearts?

704. According to the parable of the soils in Luke 8, Jesus said three things in life choke away the word of God. What are they?

705. Jesus said no one lights a lamp and puts it where?

706. Who did Jesus say were really his family?

707. When Jesus calmed the storm, what two things did his disciples say he could command?

708. In what region did they encounter the demon-possessed man?

709. Where did the demon-possessed man make his home?

710. What had the demon-possessed man broken many times to get free?

711. What did the demon say his name was?

712. Where did the demons plead with Jesus not to be thrown into?

713. Where did the demons ask to be sent?

714. How did the people of the region respond to Jesus' healing the demon-possessed man?

715. What did Jesus tell the demon-possessed man to do?

716. Who was the synagogue leader who asked Jesus to heal his daughter?

717. How old was Jairus' daughter?

718. Which three apostles entered the house and witnessed Jesus bring the girl back to life?

719. How many years had the adult woman been bleeding?

720. What article of Jesus' clothing did she touch and was healed?

721. Jesus knew he had been touched because he felt what leave him?

722. Jesus told the mourners the girl was not dead but what?

723. What five things did Jesus tell the Twelve not to take with them when they went out on the journey?

724. If people did not welcome them into a city, Jesus said to shake what off their feet?

725. When Herod the tetrarch heard about all that was going on, he was perplexed because he heard who had risen from the dead?

726. According to Luke 9, in what town did the feeding of the 5,000 occur?

727. What quantities of bread and fish did the feeding of the 5,000 begin with?

728. Who was counted during the feeding of the 5,000?

729. When Jesus fed the 5,000, he had them sit in groups of what?

730. How many basketfuls of broken pieces were left over after the feeding of the 5,000?

731. Jesus asked his followers who people said that he was. What three rumors did his disciples hear?

732. According to Jesus in Luke 9, what will happen if someone tries to save their life?

733. According to Jesus in Luke 9, how will the Son of Man react if someone is ashamed of him?

734. Who did Jesus take with him up to the mountain where the transfiguration occurred?

735. When Jesus transfigured, what does Luke 9 say his clothes became as bright as?

736. What two Old Testament figures appeared with Jesus on the Mount of his transfiguration?

737. The apostles were described as getting sleepy two times in the Gospels. Where were they?

738. What did Peter want to build for Jesus, Moses, and Elijah?

739. What three scary symptoms did the demon-possessed boy show?

740. What were the disciples arguing about when Jesus rebuked them?

741. When rejected at a Samaritan village, what did James and John want to call down from heaven?

742. Jesus said, "Foxes have holes and birds of the air have nests," but what didn't Jesus have?

743. How many did the Lord appoint and send out in groups of two?

744. In Luke 10, Jesus said the harvest is plentiful but what are there few of?

745. Jesus said he was sending them out like lambs among what other animals?

746. What three items did Jesus tell them not to bring with them in Luke 10?

747. To those unreceptive towns, what did Jesus say the disciples should wipe from their feet?

748. What three towns did Jesus warn not to reject his disciples?

749. What three Old Testament towns did Jesus say would have been more receptive to the miracles he had performed?

750. Who did the disciples say submitted to them in Jesus' name?

751. Who did Jesus see fall like lightning?

752. What two things did Jesus say they could trample on and not be harmed?

753. What two groups of people from the past did Jesus say wanted to see what his disciples were presently seeing?

754. In the parable of the good Samaritan, the man was traveling from Jerusalem to what city?

755. According to the parable of the good Samaritan, who were the two that passed by the wounded man?

756. What two liquids did the Samaritan pour on the wounds of the man?

757. How much did the Samaritan pay the innkeeper?

758. Which of the two sisters, Mary or Martha, sat at Jesus' feet while the other one worked?

759. Jesus told a parable of a persistent late-night friend who knocked on the door to borrow something. What did he want to borrow?

760. Jesus asked the fathers whether they would give their son a scorpion if the son asked for what?

761. In Luke 11, people thought Jesus drove out demons in the name of the prince of demons. What name did they give that prince of demons?

762. According to Jesus, when a demon found a man's house swept clean, how many more spirits did it invite to live there?

763. What was the only sign that this evil and wicked generation would receive according to Jesus?

764. According to Jesus, what queen would rise up in judgment against this wicked generation because she traveled so far to seek out Solomon's wisdom?

765. According to Jesus, what Old Testament city repented and yet this generation refused to repent?

766. According to Jesus, what is the lamp of the body?

767. When the Pharisee invited Jesus over for dinner, what did he notice Jesus didn't do first?

768. What two items did Jesus point out that Pharisees love to clean the outside of?

769. What two things did Pharisees love that happened in the synagogues and the marketplace?

770. What two Old Testament men did Jesus say this generation would be responsible for their deaths?

771. Whose yeast, according to Jesus, was hypocrisy?

772. Jesus said to fear those who can kill the body and throw it where?

773. In Luke 12, how many sparrows did Jesus say were sold for two pennies?

774. According to Jesus, what part of our body is numbered?

775. Jesus said anyone who blasphemed against the Son of Man would be forgiven, but anyone who blasphemed against whom would not?

776. A man's life, Jesus said, did not consist of an abundance of what?

777. In the parable of the rich fool, what did the man tear down and build bigger ones?

778. Jesus compared Solomon's clothing to what vegetation when talking about worry?

779. What vegetation, according to Jesus, is here today and tomorrow thrown in the fire?

780. According to Jesus, where a person's treasure is, what else can be found there?

781. According to Jesus, if much has been given to you, how much is demanded of you?

782. In Luke 12, Jesus said he didn't come to bring peace, but what instead?

783. According to Jesus, he will cause division between a mother-in-law and who else?

784. What did Jesus say people know how to interpret but fail to see the signs of the time?

785. Jesus spoke of a tower at Siloam that fell. How many died there?

786. Jesus healed a woman crippled by a spirit for how many years?

787. In Luke 13, what work did Jesus say the Pharisees did on the Sabbath and it didn't seem to be a problem?

788. According to Jesus, what kind of small seed was the kingdom of God like?

789. Jesus compared Herod to what animal?

790. What city did Jesus say he longed to gather together like a hen gathers its chicks?

791. In Luke 14, while Jesus ate at a prominent Pharisee's house, what illness was the man suffering from whom Jesus healed on the Sabbath?

792. What two examples did Jesus use of a person falling into a well and someone rescuing them even on the Sabbath?

793. When dining at a wedding feast, where did Jesus recommend a humble person to sit?

794. What four groups of people did Jesus say to invite to a banquet instead of family and the rich?

795. In the parable of the wedding banquet, what did the first person say he had just bought, and he used it as an excuse for not attending the banquet?

796. How many yoke of oxen did the second person say he just bought and used as an excuse for not attending the banquet?

797. Where in town did the master first tell the servant to go look for others to invite?

798. What was the second place the master told the servant to go and invite people to the banquet?

799. What must one be willing to carry to be Jesus' disciple?

800. What structure did Jesus use as an example of something one builds and estimates the cost first?

801. If salt loses its saltiness, what two places was it not fit to be thrown on?

802. The parable of the lost sheep, lost coin and lost son are found in only what Gospel?

803. Who did Jesus tell the parable of the lost sheep, coin and son to?

804. In Jesus' parable about the sheep, a man left how many sheep to find one lost one?

805. How did the shepherd in the parable carry the lost sheep home?

806. Where will there be much rejoicing over one sinner who repents?

807. In the parable of the lost coin, the woman had how many coins before she lost one?

808. What kind of coins did she have?

809. Was the son who left in the parable of the lost son older or younger than his brother who stayed at home?

810. What did the lost son spend his money on?

811. What disaster struck that made the lost son's life more difficult?

812. What animals did the lost son grow jealous of because they had food?

813. What three things did the father put on the son when he arrived home?

814. What did the older son hear that caused him to come in from the fields?

815. The older son was upset because the father never even gave him what animal?

816. The father celebrated the return of his son because he was once lost but now he was what?

817. In the parable of the shrewd manager, what product on the debtor's bill did the shrewd manager cut in half?

818. In the parable Jesus told, the shrewd manager cut the bill for one thousand bushels of wheat down to what?

819. What two masters did Jesus say we cannot serve at the same time?

820. What did Jesus say was easier to pass away before the least stroke of the pen to drop out of the Law?

821. In the story of the rich man and Lazarus, what color robe did the rich man wear?

822. What animals licked Lazarus' sores?

823. What Old Testament figure did Lazarus rest next to after he died?

824. What did the rich man want Lazarus to do to cool his tongue?

825. In the story of the rich man and Lazarus, who did the rich man ask to visit his brothers so they would believe?

826. How many brothers did the rich man have?

827. According to Abraham, who did the rich man's brothers refuse to listen to?

828. What did Jesus say it would be better to have tied around one's neck than to cause a little one to stumble?

829. If someone sinned against you seven times and repented seven times, how many times did Jesus say you are to forgive that person?

830. Jesus said one's faith need only be as big as what kind of seed?

831. What kind of tree did Jesus say in Luke 17 that your faith could toss into the sea?

832. How many lepers did Jesus heal in Luke 17?

833. Where was the healed leper from who thanked Jesus?

834. What two Old Testament people who faced devastation did Jesus compare to the coming "days of the Son of Man"?

835. In Luke 17, when Jesus talked about the day of the Son of Man, at what two places will people be when one will be taken and the other remain?

836. In Luke 17, what did Jesus say will gather where a dead body lays?

837. In the parable of the persistent widow, who was described as someone who neither feared God nor cared about man?

838. In the parable of the pharisee and tax collector, the Pharisee was thankful he was not like the tax collector and three other types of men. Who were they?

839. Jesus said we must receive the kingdom of God like who?

840. What did Jesus tell the rich young ruler he needed to do?

841. Jesus said it's more difficult for a camel to get through the eye of a needle than for who to get into heaven?

842. What physical problem was the beggar dealing with on the side of the road when Jesus asked him, "What do you want me to do for you?"

843. In what town did Zacchaeus live?

844. What was Zacchaeus' job title?

845. How was Zacchaeus' stature described?

846. What kind of a tree did Zacchaeus climb to see Jesus?

847. After meeting Jesus, Zacchaeus promised to pay back those he cheated how many times the amount?

848. As a result of Zacchaeus' actions, what did Jesus say came to Zacchaeus' house?

849. How many servants received minas in the parable of the minas?

850. In the parable of the minas, how many minas did each receive?

851. By multiplying ten minas, what was the servant put in charge of?

852. What happened to the ten minas that the wicked servant buried?

853. On what hill was Jesus standing when he gave his disciples instructions to prepare his entry into Jerusalem?

854. Why was the colt Jesus was going to ride into Jerusalem unique?

855. What did the disciples put on the colt before Jesus rode it?

856. Jesus told the Pharisees that if the disciples kept quiet, what would cry out instead?

857. What did Jesus see that made him weep as he approached Jerusalem?

858. Jesus said the temple was not a house of prayer but had become a den for who?

859. When questioned about his authority, Jesus asked whether John's baptism was from one of what two places?

860. In the parable of the tenants, the tenants beat the servants sent to collect but eventually killed whom?

861. What did Jesus say that people rejected yet it would eventually fall on them and crush them?

862. What was the value of coin that Jesus asked the spies to tell him whose portrait was on it?

863. Whose portrait was on the coin Jesus asked them to look at?

864. Which group of Jesus' enemies did not believe in the resurrection?

865. In the Sadducees' resurrection question, how many brothers were in the example?

866. Who in heaven did Jesus say never marries?

867. Whose houses did Jesus say that the Pharisees devour?

868. What did Jesus say the Pharisees do for show?

869. How many copper coins did the poor widow give?

870. Jesus said the apostles would know the desolation was near when what city was surrounded?

871. What two group of women did Jesus say it would be dreadful for during the desolation?

872. Where did Jesus say signs would appear during that devastating time mentioned in Luke 21?

873. In Luke 21, Jesus said heaven and earth would pass away, but what would never pass away?

874. Which one of the twelve apostles did satan enter?

875. On what day was the Passover lamb sacrificed?

876. Which two apostles did Jesus send to prepare the Passover feast?

877. What was the man carrying who led the disciples to the house where the Last Supper would occur?

878. Jesus said he would drink the fruit of the vine when what finally comes?

879. What was the argument over at the Last Supper?

880. Who did satan ask to sift like wheat?

881. What two places did Peter say he was willing to go for Jesus?

882. Jesus predicted that the rooster would crow before Peter denied Jesus how many times?

883. What did Jesus tell his disciples to purchase at the Last Supper if they didn't already have one?

884. What two weapons did the disciples show Jesus they were carrying at the Last Supper?

885. Upon reaching the Mount of Olives, Jesus told his disciples to pray that they weren't led into what?

886. In Luke 22, as Jesus prayed in the garden, what did Jesus ask that his Father take from him?

887. In Luke 22, what was Jesus' sweat like as it dripped to the ground?

888. Which ear of the servant's high priest was cut off in the garden of Gethsemane?

889. What did Jesus do with the dismembered ear?

890. Who first accused Peter of associating with Jesus?

891. Who looked straight at Peter after his third denial in the courtyard?

892. What two identities did the council of elders ask Jesus if he believed he was?

893. In Luke 23, what two accusations against Jesus did the chief priests bring?

894. Because Jesus was a Galilean, to whom did Pilate send him as part of the trial?

895. What did Herod hope the arrested Jesus would perform for him?

896. Because of Jesus' trial, what two leaders became friends?

897. Who did the people want released instead of Jesus?

898. Why had Barabbas been thrown into jail?

899. Who did the soldiers seize and force to carry Jesus' cross?

900. How did the guards decide who would receive Jesus' clothes?

901. What did the guards offer Jesus to drink at his crucifixion?

902. What did the sign above Jesus read on the cross?

903. Where did Jesus tell the one criminal he would go that day?

904. According to Luke 23, how many hours did darkness come over the whole land during Jesus' crucifixion?

905. What in the temple tore into two?

906. Who watched Jesus die and said, "Surely this was a righteous man"?

907. From what town was Joseph, the member of the council, who buried Jesus?

908. What two items did the women go home and prepare for Jesus' burial?

909. In the Luke 24 account, how many angels did Luke mention were inside the tomb?

910. What did the men's clothes gleam like?

911. Name the three women who reported Jesus' resurrection.

912. To what village were the two men traveling when Jesus met them?

913. How far was Emmaus from Jerusalem?

914. What was the name of one of the men on the road to Emmaus?

915. What food item did Jesus eat with them?

916. What action did Jesus do immediately before the traveling disciples recognized it was Jesus?

917. When Jesus appeared in the room with the disciples, what did they first think he was?

918. Jesus told them that a ghost didn't have what two things?

919. What food item did Jesus eat in the upper room after his resurrection?

920. When Jesus appeared to the disciples, what did he open so they could understand the Scriptures?

921. Jesus told them to stay in the city until they were clothed with what?

922. In the vicinity of what town did Jesus ascend?

923. What did the disciples do afterwards, continually, in the temple?

John

924. John 1:1 begins with the same three words as what other book of the Bible?

925. John 1 says the light shines, but what can't overcome it?

926. According to John 1, who was the man sent from God as a witness concerning the light?

927. To those that believe in the one who came into the world, what did they receive the right to become?

928. What did the Word become in order to make his dwelling among us?

929. John 1 says the law came from Moses, but what two things came through Jesus?

930. What three identities did the Jewish leaders ask if John was (and he denied)?

931. What prophet did John quote back to the Jewish leaders when asked who he was?

932. What of Jesus' did John say he was not worthy to untie?

933. In what city was John baptizing according to John 1?

934. When John saw Jesus, he called him the Lamb of God who takes away what?

935. What did John say he saw descending like a dove on the Chosen One?

936. Which soon-to-be apostle heard John call Jesus the Lamb of God?

937. Who did this apostle then bring to Jesus to introduce them?

938. What name did Jesus give Simon?

939. What town were Philip, Peter and Andrew from?

940. Who couldn't believe anything good came out of Nazareth?

941. Which apostle invited Nathanael to meet Jesus?

942. Where did Jesus say he saw Nathanael sitting?

943. What did Jesus tell Nathanael he would see ascending and descending on the Son of Man?

944. In what town was the wedding held where Jesus turned the water into wine?

945. In what region of Israel was the town of Cana located?

946. After how many days did the wedding run out of wine?

947. How many stone water jars did Jesus fill when he changed water to wine?

948. When Jesus changed the water to wine, how many gallons did each stone jar hold?

949. Who first tasted the wine that Jesus miraculously changed?

950. What three animals were mentioned when Jesus cleared the temple?

951. When Jesus cleared the temple, what did he make out of cords?

952. When the Jews asked for a sign, Jesus said he would raise up a destroyed temple in how many days?

953. How many years did the Jews tell Jesus it took to build the temple?

954. What "temple" did the disciples realize later Jesus meant?

955. Who was the Jewish leader that came to Jesus at night in John 3?

956. What was his title?

957. How did Nicodemus know Jesus was from God and God was with him?

958. Jesus told Nicodemus that the only way you can see the kingdom of heaven was to be what?

959. What did Nicodemus find it hard to enter a second time in order to be born again?

960. Jesus likened the Spirit to what weather condition?

961. Jesus compared the Son of Man's "lifting up" to Moses lifting up what in the wilderness?

962. John 3:17 said God did not send the Son into the world to do what?

963. John 3 said those who hate light are afraid what will be exposed?

964. In John 3, John was baptizing near where?

965. Who said, "He must become greater; I must become less"?

966. John 4 says Jesus did not baptize, but who did instead?

967. In John 4, Jesus met the woman at the well in what town near the plot of ground Jacob gave to his son Joseph in Samaria?

968. What did Jesus tell the Samaritan woman would happen to everyone who drank the water she pulled from the well?

969. What did Jesus tell the Samaritan woman would happen to everyone who drank the water he gave them?

970. How many husbands did Jesus say the woman at the well previously had in addition to the man she currently had?

971. In John 4, Jesus said the time was coming when the true worshippers would worship in _____ and _____.

972. What is the other word for Messiah that appeared in John 4:25?

973. What did the woman at the well leave behind to go tell the people that she had seen the Messiah?

974. What was Jesus' "food" as he explained to his disciples?

975. Jesus told his disciples to open their eyes because the harvest was in what condition?

976. In what city did the royal official's son whom Jesus healed lay sick and dying?

977. In what city was Jesus when he healed the royal official's son?

978. In what city does the gospel of John connect the first two miracles of Jesus?

979. In John 4, what does John say was the second miracle?

980. What was the Aramaic name of the Sheep Gate pool?

981. How many covered colonnades surrounded the pool of Bethesda?

982. How many years was the man by the pool paralyzed?

983. What was the man waiting for by the pool of Bethesda?

984. What did the religious leaders say the once-paralyzed man did to break the Sabbath law?

985. What was Jesus calling God that made the religious leaders upset?

986. According to Jesus in John 5, where will people be when they hear his voice and come out?

987. According to Jesus in John 5, which man's testimony validated who Jesus was?

988. What did Jesus say the Pharisees diligently studied because they thought they had eternal life?

989. What Old Testament figure did Jesus say wrote about him?

990. What is another name for the Sea of Tiberias?

991. According to John 6, who was the apostle Jesus asked "Where are we going to buy bread for these people to eat?"

992. According to the apostles, what amount of wages were not enough to buy food for the 5,000?

993. Who brought up the boy with the fish and bread during the feeding of the 5,000?

994. How much food did the boy have on him?

995. What grain was the bread made of that fed the 5,000?

996. How many baskets were left over from the feeding of the 5,000?

997. What did Jesus believe the people were going to force him to become?

998. About how many miles offshore were the disciples when they saw Jesus walking on water?

999. What miracle in John 6 prompted Jesus to talk about being the Bread of Life?

1000. In John 6, what Old Testament hero's bread-producing ability did Jesus compare himself to?

1001. In John 6, Jesus called himself the _____ of Life.

1002. What two things did Jesus say people must eat and drink to have eternal life?

1003. When Jesus called one of his twelve a devil, whom was he talking about?

1004. What was the name of Judas' father?

1005. What feast did Jesus' unbelieving brothers encourage him to go to?

1006. What patriarchal ceremony did Jesus point out that the Pharisees performed on the Sabbath, yet they got upset at him when he did a miracle on the Sabbath?

1007. According to Jesus, what will flow from a man who believes in Him?

1008. What did Jesus really mean would flow from believers in that statement but they would receive it later?

1009. In John 7, the people struggled with thinking the Messiah would not come from what region?

1010. In John 7, who failed to arrest Jesus, irritating the chief priests?

1011. What story in John 8 only appears in the Gospel of John and does not appear in all of the ancient manuscripts?

1012. After being questioned about the woman caught in adultery, what did Jesus bend over to the ground to do?

1013. What did Jesus say those without sin could throw?

1014. In John 8, Jesus verified his identity because of the testimony of two witnesses. Who were those two witnesses?

1015. What did Jesus say would set someone free once they knew it?

1016. Who did the Pharisees believe their father was?

1017. Who did Jesus say the Pharisees were the children of?

1018. In John 8, Jesus said those who obey his word will never see what?

1019. In John 8:58, Jesus claimed to exist before what Old Testament patriarch, causing the religious leaders to pick up stones to stone him?

1020. Why did Jesus believe the man was born blind?

1021. What did Jesus mix together before he put it in the eyes of the blind man at Siloam?

1022. In what pool did the man born blind wash his eyes?

1023. What does the word *Siloam* mean?

1024. Why did the Pharisees tell the once-blind man that the person who healed him was not from God?

1025. Who did the Pharisees send for to hear more information about the man born blind?

1026. What were the Jewish leaders willing to kick people out of if they believed Jesus was the Messiah?

1027. The now-healed blind man said, "One thing I know, I was _____ but now I _____."

1028. According to Jesus' parable, the sheep know the shepherd because they recognize what?

1029. Which two of Jesus' "I Am" statements in John have to do with sheep?

1030. When talking about the Good Shepherd, Jesus said the hired hand runs away in fear from what animal?

1031. What did Jesus say he had the authority to lay down and take up again?

1032. The Jews got upset because Jesus said he and who else were one?

1033. What were the Jewish leaders going to do to Jesus because they felt he blasphemed?

1034. John 11 says Lazarus, Mary, and Martha were from what village?

1035. John points out that this Mary was the same one who previously showed her affection to Jesus by doing what?

1036. How many more days did Jesus stay where he was when he heard Lazarus was sick?

1037. What term did Jesus use to describe Lazarus' condition even though others said he was dead?

1038. John pointed out that Thomas went by another name. What was it?

1039. When Jesus found Lazarus, how many days had Lazarus been in the tomb?

1040. How far (in miles) was Bethany from Jerusalem?

1041. Which sister, Mary or Martha or both, knew that if Jesus had been around, Lazarus would not have died?

1042. Which sister, Mary or Martha or both, said that Lazarus would rise again on resurrection day?

1043. The death of what friend caused Jesus to say. "I am the resurrection and the life"?

1044. The shortest verse of the New Testament, "Jesus wept," described Jesus' reaction during the death of whom?

1045. What phrase did Jesus yell to raise Lazarus from the dead?

1046. What was Lazarus wrapped in as he came out of the tomb?

1047. Which high priest prophesied that it was better for one man to die for the people than the whole nation to perish?

1048. According to John 12, who poured perfume on Jesus' feet and wiped them with her hair?

1049. The perfume was described as a pint of what?

1050. Who objected to this act, believing the money could go to other uses like helping the poor?

1051. Who did he think the money could go to?

1052. Who was the keeper of the money bag among the disciples?

1053. Why did the writer call Judas a thief?

1054. Besides Jesus, who else did the chief priests want to kill because people were putting their faith in Christ?

1055. What Old Testament prophet foresaw the coming of a king on a donkey?

1056. Which apostle did the Greeks come to for an audience with Jesus?

1057. In John 12, when Jesus talked about a kernel falling to the ground and dying, what kind of kernel was it?

1058. What Old Testament prophet did the writer of John believe foresaw people's blindness and dead hearts during the time of Jesus?

1059. In John 12, what did the Pharisees love more than praise from God?

1060. At the Last Supper, who did satan prompt to betray Jesus, according to John 13?

1061. When Jesus washed the disciples' feet, what did he wrap around his waist first?

1062. Who rejected Jesus' offer to wash his feet?

1063. What other two parts of the body did Peter ask Jesus to wash besides just his feet?

1064. What did Jesus hand his betrayer to indicate his identity at the Last Supper?

1065. Who did he hand the bread to?

1066. Who is Judas Iscariot's father?

1067. Who entered Judas, encouraging him to betray Jesus?

1068. Who was in charge of the money at the Last Supper?

1069. What "new command" did Jesus give his disciples at the Last Supper?

1070. Jesus predicted Peter would deny him three times before what bird crowed?

1071. What did Jesus say in John 14 that he was going off to prepare for those who trusted in him?

1072. Jesus said, "I am the _____, the _____, and the _____."

1073. Which apostle asked Jesus in John 14, "Lord show us the father"?

1074. In John 14, what evidence did Jesus feel he provided to make his case that he and the Father were one?

1075. Who was the Counselor/Advocate Jesus spoke about in John 14?

1076. What did Jesus say he gives, but not like the way the world offers it?

1077. Since Jesus is the vine, what is the Father?

1078. What does the Father do to the branches that bear no fruit?

1079. What does the Father do to the branches that bear fruit?

1080. Since Jesus is the vine, what are we?

1081. What did Jesus ask us to bear much of in John 15?

1082. What is the greatest love man can show, according to Jesus in John 15?

1083. Since Jesus calls us friends, we are no longer called what?

1084. Who will the Father send to testify about the truth of the Son?

1085. Jesus said he needed to go away so who would come to the disciples?

1086. What three things would the Holy Spirit convict the world of?

1087. What did Jesus say a pregnant woman forgets once the baby is born?

1088. What did Jesus say in John 16 that he has overcome?

1089. In John 17, Jesus prayed that none were lost except the one doomed to what?

1090. After praying in John 17, what valley did Jesus cross with his disciples before his arrest?

1091. Why did Judas know that Jesus would be in the olive garden?

1092. What three items were Jesus' arresting party carrying in John 18?

1093. What happened to the arresting party in Gethsemane after the first time Jesus said "I am he"?

1094. Who drew a sword at Gethsemane and cut off an ear?

1095. Which of the servant's ears was cut off?

1096. Who did the servant belong to?

1097. What was the name of the servant whose ear was cut off?

1098. According to John 18, who was the first person the soldiers brought Jesus to after the arrest?

1099. Who was his father-in-law?

1100. Who was the first person to accuse Peter of being associated with Jesus?

1101. Where was Peter standing during his first denial?

1102. What were Peter and the officials standing around when Peter was first accused?

1103. According to John 18, who was the second person Jesus was brought to after the arrest?

1104. Peter was accused of being Jesus' disciple by a relative of whom?

1105. The Jews did not enter Pilate's palace or risk ceremonial uncleanness before what holiday?

1106. Who said, "What is truth?"

1107. Who did the crowd want released instead of Jesus?

1108. What kind of a criminal act did Barabbas take part in according to John 18?

1109. What did the soldiers make Jesus' crown out of?

1110. What color robe did the soldiers put on Jesus while they beat and mocked him?

1111. Who presented a beaten Jesus to the crowd and said, "Here is the man!"?

1112. Who did the Jews accuse Pilate of not being a friend to?

1113. What is the name of the place where the judge's seat was located?

1114. What was the name of the judge's seat area in Aramaic?

1115. During Jesus' trial, who did the chief priests claim to be their king?

1116. What is the name of the place where Jesus carried his cross?

1117. What is the name of that place in Aramaic?

1118. In what three languages was the sign written that hung over Jesus' head during the crucifixion?

1119. Into how many parts did the soldiers divide Jesus' clothes?

1120. What possession of Jesus' at the crucifixion was seamless, all in one piece?

1121. Which part of Jesus' clothing did they not tear?

1122. John mentioned three women by the cross who all shared what name?

1123. Who were the three women mentioned in John 19 that were at the crucifixion?

1124. While on the cross, who did Jesus present to his mother as her son?

1125. What drink was Jesus offered on the cross?

1126. What did they soak it in?

1127. How did they lift it to Jesus' lips?

1128. What part of Jesus' body did they not break on the cross?

1129. Who pierced Jesus in his side?

1130. What two liquids flowed out of Jesus after he was pierced on the cross?

1131. Who asked Pilate for Jesus' body?

1132. How many pounds of myrrh and aloes did Nicodemus bring?

1133. In John 20, who alerted the apostles that the tomb was empty?

1134. According to John 20, which apostle entered the tomb first?

1135. What were the only two material items left inside Jesus' empty tomb?

1136. According to John 20, what two people did Mary see in the tomb?

1137. What color were they dressed in?

1138. John 20 says Mary Magdalene mistook Jesus for whom?

1139. According to John 20, who spoke to the resurrected Jesus first?

1140. When she realized it was Jesus, what Aramaic term did she cry out?

1141. Who were the disciples afraid of after the death of Jesus, so they hid behind locked doors?

1142. When the risen Jesus visited the disciples in the locked upper room, what phrase did he say three times in John 20?

1143. What two scarred parts of Jesus' body did he tell Thomas to see and touch?

1144. After Thomas demanded to see Jesus' nail marks and side, how long afterward did Jesus show up?

1145. What did Thomas say after he saw the risen Christ?

1146. What was the other name Thomas went by?

1147. Where was the apostle Nathanael from?

1148. What two food items had Jesus prepared for his apostles on the shoreline in John 21?

1149. How many fish were in the nets after the miraculous catch of fish in John 21?

1150. When Jesus met the disciples on the shore of the Sea of Galilee, how many total times had he appeared to them after the resurrection?

1151. How many times did Jesus ask Peter to either feed or take care of his sheep and lambs?

1152. Because of Jesus' statements at the end of John 21, which two apostles' deaths were speculated?

1153. The Gospel of John ends by saying there was not enough what to contain all the stories about Jesus?

Acts

1154. To whom did Luke write the Book of Acts?

1155. The book of Acts said that Jesus appeared to his apostles for how many days after the resurrection?

1156. In Acts 1, Jesus told his followers while eating not to leave what city?

1157. In Acts 1, Jesus said that John baptized with water, but Jesus would baptize them with what in a few days?

1158. In Acts 1, Jesus told his followers they would be his witnesses in what four places?

1159. When Jesus ascended in Acts 1, how many men in white showed up?

1160. What did these men in white wonder what the followers were standing around and looking at?

1161. What was the name of the mountain where they watched Jesus ascend into heaven?

1162. Who of Jesus' family joined the apostles in prayer after the ascension?

1163. About how many people were with Peter when he first stood and addressed the group in the book of Acts?

1164. How does Acts 1 say Judas died?

1165. What was the name given to the field where Judas died?

1166. What two men were considered to replace Judas the apostle?

1167. What were the two other names for Barsabbas in Acts 1?

1168. How was the replacement apostle chosen in Acts 1?

1169. What was the name of the apostle chosen to replace Judas?

1170. During what festival did the disciples of Jesus speak in other tongues?

1171. What did the arrival of the Holy Spirit sound like at Pentecost?

1172. What kind of structure were the disciples in when the Holy Spirit arrived at Pentecost?

1173. What seemed to rest on the heads of each of them at Pentecost?

1174. What region did the crowd know the tongue-speakers were originally from?

1175. What did the witnesses of the Pentecostal tongue miracle think the participants had too much of?

1176. Which apostle stood up during Pentecost in Acts 2 and spoke to the crowd?

1177. What time of the day did Peter say it was when the miracle of Pentecost happened, which was too early to get drunk?

1178. When Peter addressed the crowd after this incident, who was the first Old Testament writer that he quoted?

1179. What did this prophet say God would pour out in these last days?

1180. Peter went on during his speech in Acts 2 and quoted David twice from what book of the Bible?

1181. In Acts 2, Peter told the people to repent and then to do what?

1182. How many new believers were added after Peter's speech on Pentecost?

1183. As the church grew, what were the people selling to help others in need?

1184. In Acts 3, what was the name of the gate were Peter and John healed a crippled man?

1185. What did the crippled man want but Peter gave him healing instead?

1186. Peter said in Acts 3 that all the prophets since which two men have foretold of the coming of Jesus?

1187. By Acts 4, the number of men who heard and believed the message grew to what number?

1188. Which two apostles did Annas and Caiaphas have brought before them?

1189. What did Annas, Caiaphas, and the others realize about Peter and John and it astonished them?

1190. How old was the crippled man that Peter and John healed?

1191. After the believers prayed in Acts 4, what happened to the place where they were praying?

1192. What other name was Joseph, a Levite from Cyprus, known by in Acts 4?

1193. What did his other name mean?

1194. What did he sell in order to bring the money to the apostles?

1195. Who was Sapphira's husband?

1196. What did Ananias and Sapphira sell and bring a portion of the sale to the apostles' feet?

1197. Who did Peter say filled Ananias' heart?

1198. Who did Peter say Ananias and Sapphira lied to?

1199. What happened to Ananias that caused great fear?

1200. How much later did Sapphira enter the room after Ananias?

1201. What did Peter predict would happen to Sapphira and it came true?

1202. By Acts 5, where did the believers meet together on a regular basis?

1203. In Acts 5, whose shadow did people hope would fall on the sick to heal them?

1204. Who opened the jail cell doors and let the arrested apostles out?

1205. As soon as the apostles were released, where did the angel have them go and preach?

1206. Who was the Pharisee that stood and defended the apostles, saying this movement would die out like the others?

1207. Name the two leaders of past religious movements that he mentioned.

1208. Because of Gamaliel's speech, the apostles were not killed but what was done to them instead?

1209. Who complained that their widows were being overlooked during food distribution to the needy?

1210. How many men were chosen to wait on tables?

1211. Who were the seven that were chosen?

1212. Of the seven that were chosen, which one was described as full of faith and the Holy Spirit?

1213. What was the name of the group that argued with Stephen and conspired to have him arrested?

1214. After Stephen was seized, who was he brought before on trial?

1215. Those who looked at Stephen said his face was like a what?

1216. In Acts 7, Stephen talked about three periods of Moses' life that all lasted how many years each?

1217. In Acts 7, what did the Sanhedrin gnash while Stephen talked?

1218. Who did Stephen look to the heavens and see?

1219. While Stephen spoke, what did their Sanhedrin cover while yelling at the top of their voices?

1220. Who did the participants of Stephen's death lay their cloaks at the feet of?

1221. Since a persecution broke out against the church in Jerusalem, to what two places did people scatter?

1222. After Stephen's death, who began to go house to house and try to destroy the church?

1223. In Acts 8, what region did Philip first travel to and preach the good news?

1224. What was the name of the sorcerer in Acts 8 who became a believer?

1225. Which apostle did Simon the Sorcerer follow after believing in God?

1226. When the apostles heard that the people in Samaria accepted the word of God, who did they send there to check it out?

1227. What did Simon offer to the apostles in order to receive the Holy Spirit?

1228. An angel led Philip to a road to Gaza in order to meet who?

1229. What was the Ethiopian eunuch in charge of?

1230. What book of the Bible was the Ethiopian eunuch reading when Philip found him?

1231. What was the Ethiopian eunuch sitting in when Philip ran up to him?

1232. What did the Ethiopian eunuch see that encouraged him to be baptized?

1233. After Philip baptized the Ethiopian eunuch, what city did he suddenly appear in?

1234. Philip preached the gospel in all the towns until he reached what city?

1235. What city was Saul heading toward when a light flashed from heaven?

1236. What was the first name given for this movement of Christianity?

1237. Who spoke to Paul from heaven on this road?

1238. As a result of the encounter, which of Saul's senses did he lose?

1239. For how many days did he lose this sense?

1240. Who was the man in Damascus that the Lord asked to go pray for Saul?

1241. In whose house was Saul staying at the time?

1242. On what street was the house?

1243. What city was Paul from?

1244. After Ananias' prayed for Saul, something like what fell from Saul's eyes?

1245. After Saul's sight was restored, what was the next thing he did?

1246. How was Saul lowered over the city wall to escape the Jews?

1247. Who brought Saul to the apostles?

1248. Who did Saul talk and debate with but they tried to kill him?

1249. What was the name of the paralytic Peter healed that had been bedridden for eight years?

1250. What was the name of the disciple who always did good and helped the poor that Peter raised from the dead?

1251. In Acts 9, who was the tanner Peter stayed with in Joppa?

1252. Who was the centurion in Caesarea that had a vision about Peter?

1253. What regiment did Cornelius come from?

1254. At whose house was Peter staying when he had his vision?

1255. What did Peter see that was let down from heaven by its four corners?

1256. What kind of animals were in Peter's vision?

1257. How many times did the vision repeat itself?

1258. At Cornelius' house, Peter told the group that it was against religious law for a Jew to associate with whom?

1259. Whose persecution caused believers to scatter as far as Phoenicia, Cyprus, and Antioch?

1260. Where did Barnabas find Saul in Acts 11?

1261. In what city were the disciples first called Christians?

1262. Name the prophet who predicted the famine in Acts 11.

1263. During which emperor's reign did this famine occur?

1264. Which king had James the brother of John put to death?

1265. How was James the brother of John killed?

1266. Who did Peter say the Lord sent to rescue him from Herod's clutches?

1267. Whose house did Peter go to once he was freed from jail?

1268. Who was the servant girl who answered the door when Peter was released from prison?

1269. When Peter was at the door after being miraculously released, who did the people think it really was?

1270. Because of Peter's escape from prison, who did Herod have executed?

1271. Who had Herod been quarreling with before he made his speech?

1272. What did the passage say Herod had on when he made his speech?

1273. Why did Herod (Agrippa I) die in Acts 12?

1274. How did Herod (Agrippa I) die in Acts 12?

1275. Herod died, but what does the passage say happened to the word of God?

1276. After Saul and Barnabas returned from Jerusalem, who did they take with them in Acts 12?

1277. What two people from the church in Antioch did the Holy Spirit want for a mission trip?

1278. Who joined Paul and Barnabas on their first missionary journey then left them in Perga?

1279. What was the name of the Jewish sorcerer and false prophet Paul and Barnabas met?

1280. Who was the proconsul in Paphos who wanted to hear the word of God?

1281. What did the name Elymas mean?

1282. What affliction was Elymas the sorcerer struck with after meeting Paul?

1283. Where did John leave Paul and Barnabas and return to Jerusalem?

1284. According to Paul in Acts 13, how many nations did God overthrow to settle the Israelites in Canaan?

1285. Who was jealous about the attention Paul and Barnabas were receiving?

1286. Since the Jews rejected their message, who did Paul say he must bring the message to instead?

1287. What two groups of influential people did the Jews incite against Paul and Barnabas?

1288. According to Acts 14, when Paul entered a city, where did he usually go to speak?

1289. In Acts 14, Paul and Barnabas escaped a plot to kill them in Iconium and fled to what two cities?

1290. In Acts 14, what did the lame man have that told Paul he could be healed?

1291. What god did the people of Lystra call Barnabas?

1292. What god did the people of Lystra call Paul?

1293. After Paul was dragged outside Lystra and stoned, what did he do next?

1294. In Acts 14, who did Paul and Barnabas ordain over the churches before they returned home?

1295. What did the men from Judea teach that needed to be done before Gentiles could be saved?

1296. In Acts 15, what proof did Peter say showed that God had accepted Gentile believers (with or without circumcision)?

1297. What three New Testament writers attended the Council at Jerusalem in Acts 15?

1298. What four things did James suggest that Gentiles should abstain from?

1299. In Acts 15, what two men joined Paul and Barnabas on their trip to Antioch?

1300. Who did Barnabas want to take on a missionary journey, but Paul disagreed?

1301. After Paul and Barnabas parted ways, who did Paul take with him to Syria?

1302. Acts 16 says Timothy's mother was a Jewess and his father was a what?

1303. What did Paul need to do to Timothy before he took him on the journey?

1304. What two cities did Paul visit in Acts 16 that he later wrote letters to that are in the New Testament?

1305. What city did the Spirit of Jesus keep Paul from entering in Acts 16?

1306. Paul had a vision of a man begging him to come to his region. What region was it?

1307. Who was the woman from Thyatira who heard Paul's message in Macedonia and opened her heart?

1308. What kind of product did she deal in?

1309. How did the slave girl who followed Paul around earn a great deal of money?

1310. What were Paul and Silas doing while locked in chains in prison that the other prisoners were listening to?

1311. What caused the prison doors to fly open when Paul and Silas were in prison?

1312. What did the jailer almost do when he realized the prison doors were opened?

1313. Who ran into the jail after the earthquake and asked Paul and Silas how to be saved?

1314. Where did the jailer take them that night after his family was baptized?

1315. What fact about Paul and Silas alarmed the officers?

1316. Whose house did the mob search to look for Paul and Silas in Thessalonica?

1317. What group of people received Paul's words with eagerness and examined the Scriptures every day to see if his message was true?

1318. The Bereans had a more noble character than what other people group?

1319. What two groups of philosophers debated with Paul in Athens?

1320. In what city did Paul preach at the Areopagus?

1321. While complimenting the people for their religiousness in Athens, Paul mentioned an altar with an inscription to whom?

1322. After his speech at the Areopagus, what were the names of the man and woman who became followers of Paul?

1323. After Paul left Athens, what city did he travel to and met Aquila and Priscilla?

1324. Why did Priscilla and Aquila have to leave Rome?

1325. According to Acts 18, what was Paul's other job besides apostle?

1326. Who was the Corinthian synagogue leader in Acts 18 who believed in the Lord and his entire household?

1327. How long, according to Acts 18, did Paul spend in Corinth?

1328. What was the name of the proconsul of Achaia that the Jews in Corinth brought Paul before?

1329. What did Paul have done in Cenchreae because of a vow he had taken?

1330. In Acts 18, who did Priscilla and Aquila explain the gospel to more completely while in Ephesus?

1331. Apollos taught about Jesus but only knew about whose baptism?

1332. What had some disciples in Ephesus never heard of?

1333. What baptism had the disciples in Ephesus received before Paul arrived?

1334. What kind of baptism did Paul say was John's?

1335. What did the disciples do after Paul laid his hands on them?

1336. About how many men were present when the Holy Spirit came upon them in Ephesus?

1337. In Acts 19, how many months did Paul spend in the Ephesian synagogue speaking boldly about the kingdom of God?

1338. Where was the lecture hall that Paul had daily discussion in?

1339. Because of Paul's work in the province of Asia for two years, what two groups heard the word of the Lord?

1340. What two items that Paul touched in Acts 19 healed those they were brought to?

1341. Who was the Jewish chief priest whose seven sons tried to drive out demons but were attacked by them instead?

1342. What condition were the sons in as they ran from the house after the demon attack?

1343. What did those who once practiced sorcery burn publicly?

1344. In drachmas, what was the value of the sorcery scrolls burned by those in Ephesus?

1345. In Acts 19, which two of Paul's workers did he send to Macedonia?

1346. What was the name of the silversmith who opposed Paul in Ephesus and stirred up a riot?

1347. What did Demetrius make for Artemis?

1348. What goddess was the city of Ephesus the guardian for?

1349. Who were the two traveling companions seized by the mob in Ephesus?

1350. Who was pushed to the front to speak to the crowd, until they realized he was a Jew?

1351. How many hours did the crowd shout, "Great is Artemis of the Ephesians"?

1352. What was the job title of the person who dismissed the assembly?

1353. According to those in Ephesus, how did the image of Artemis come to the city?

1354. Where did he suggest that Demetrius and the others take up the matter?

1355. Who was the young man who fell to his death while Paul spoke?

1356. How many stories did the young man fall?

1357. Paul said goodbye to the elders from what church in chapter 20?

1358. Who did Paul quote when he said, "It is more blessed to give than to receive"?

1359. What evangelist had four unmarried daughters who prophesied?

1360. Name the prophet who wrapped Paul's belt around his hands and feet.

1361. This prophet warned Paul not to go to what city?

1362. In Acts 21, Paul's accusers where upset when they saw him enter what place?

1363. In Acts 21, who saved Paul from the riot in Jerusalem?

1364. In Acts 22, where did Paul say he was born?

1365. Who was the teacher Paul trained under in the law?

1366. What citizenship was Paul born into?

1367. Why did Paul's interrogators stop pressuring him in Acts 22?

1368. While Paul spoke to the Sanhedrin, who ordered Paul struck in the mouth?

1369. Who said that he was a Pharisee and a son of a Pharisee?

1370. What religious sect said there was no resurrection and that neither angels nor spirits existed?

1371. In what city did the Lord tell Paul he would testify about him after Jerusalem?

1372. Forty men took a vow that would not do what until Paul had been killed?

1373. Who heard of the plot to kill Paul and warned him in the barracks?

1374. After hearing about this plot, what governor did the Roman commander send Paul to for safe keeping?

1375. What was the name of the lawyer the high priest Ananias brought in to bring charges against Paul?

1376. What was the name of Governor Felix's wife, a Jewess, who listened to Paul's story?

1377. What was Felix hoping Paul would offer him, but never received?

1378. Years later, who succeeded Felix as governor and held a trial with Paul?

1379. To what city did Festus go and discuss Paul's case with the chief priests?

1380. Who did Paul appeal to during his trial with Festus?

1381. Who was the king and his wife that wanted an audience with Paul while he was in prison in Caesarea?

1382. What language did the voice speak to Paul on the road to Damascus, according to his story?

1383. What did Agrippa deny that Paul could persuade him to become in such a short time?

1384. King Agrippa felt Paul could be set free if he had not done what?

1385. What was the name of the centurion in the imperial regiment who escorted Paul and other prisoners to Rome by ship?

1386. Who was the Macedonian from Thessalonica that joined Paul on the voyage?

1387. Paul warned them that this voyage would be disastrous, but the centurion listened to whom instead?

1388. What kind of wind storm struck Paul's boat while sailing to Rome?

1389. What did the crew pass under the ship to keep it together during the storm?

1390. In Acts 27, an angel visited Paul on the ship and told him he would stand trial before who?

1391. In Acts 27, the ship ran aground while they sailed in what sea?

1392. How long hadn't the people on the ship eaten until Paul encouraged them to do so?

1393. How many people were on board Paul's ship sailing to Rome?

1394. What island did Paul reach after the shipwreck?

1395. What creature bit Paul's hand while he gathered firewood on the island?

1396. Who was the chief official on the island of Malta?

1397. Paul healed a Maltan official's father of what disease?

1398. Paul eventually left the island on a ship with what two gods as its figurehead?

1399. How long does Acts say Paul was in Rome speaking to people from his rented house?

Romans

1400. In Romans 1, what did Paul say he was set apart for?

1401. What group of people did Paul in Romans 1 say he felt called to?

1402. In Romans 1, what did Paul wish to impart on the Romans to make them strong?

1403. Paul was not ashamed of the gospel because it is the power of God that brings what to everyone who believes?

1404. What two invisible qualities about God have been clearly seen since the creation of the world?

1405. In Romans 1, what did the people exchange the glory of the immortal God for?

1406. What four things did these mortal images look like, according to Romans 1?

1407. In Romans 1, what did Paul say the people exchanged the truth about God for?

1408. What kind of a mind did those who refused to retain the knowledge of God receive in return?

1409. Paul, in Romans 2, said we who pass judgment are really condemning who?

1410. What are stubborn and unrepentant people storing up for themselves according to Romans 2?

1411. In Romans 2, Paul said God will repay each person according to what?

1412. Romans 2 says it is not those who hear the law that are considered righteous, but those who do what?

1413. Where do the Gentiles have the requirements of the law written?

1414. Paul spoke to Jews and said that they teach others, but who do they fail to teach?

1415. In Romans 2, what Jewish practice did Paul say had value if you observe the law?

1416. Romans 2 says a man is not this outwardly and physically but only inwardly?

1417. According to Paul in Romans 3, what group of people was entrusted with the very words of God?

1418. Paul argued in Romans 3 that some believe their falsehood increases God's what?

1419. Which three books of the Bible does Paul quote from in Romans 3:10-18 about our sinfulness?

1420. Romans 3:13 says people's throats are an open what?

1421. According to Romans 3:15, what part of people's bodies are swift to shed blood?

1422. According to Romans 3:23, all people fall short of what?

1423. Romans 3 says God presented Jesus as a sacrifice of atonement through faith in his what?

1424. Romans 3 says we are justified by what and not by works of the law?

1425. If someone works, according to Romans 4, their wages are not a gift but what?

1426. In Romans 4, Paul quoted Genesis 15 to say that Abraham believed God and what was credited to him?

1427. Romans 4 said that Abraham was the father of all those who had and had not performed what procedure?

1428. According to Romans 4:15, what does the law bring?

1429. According to Romans 4:15, where there is no law, there is no what?

1430. Around how old was Abraham according to Romans 4 when he faced the fact his body was as good as dead?

1431. Romans 5:1 states that since we have been justified through faith, what do we now have between us and God?

1432. Romans 5 says we get perseverance through what?

1433. According to Romans 5, what two things does perseverance eventually produce?

1434. What kind of person does Romans 5 say that someone would possibly die for?

1435. According to Romans 5:8, what did Christ do for us so that God could demonstrate his love for us sinners?

1436. According to Romans 5, how many men brought sin into the world?

1437. How many sins brought judgment and condemnation according to Romans 5?

1438. Through the obedience of how many men were many made righteous?

1439. Romans 5 says that where sin increased, what increased all the more?

1440. According to Romans 6, what should we not go on doing so that grace can increase?

1441. According to Romans 6, if we've been united with Jesus in his death, we have also been united with him in what?

1442. In Romans 6, what no longer has mastery over Christ?

1443. In Romans 6, Paul said we've been set free from sin so we can be slaves to what?

1444. If the wages of sin is death, what is the free gift of God in Christ Jesus?

1445. According to Romans 7, if a woman marries another man while her husband is alive, what is she called?

1446. In Romans 7, because of the law what do we now recognize?

1447. Apart from the law, what is dead?

1448. In Romans 7, Paul said if he did what he didn't want to do, what was living inside him?

1449. In Romans 8, the mind of sinful man is death, but the mind controlled by the Spirit is what?

1450. In Romans 8, the Spirit frees us from being what so that we no longer have to live in fear again?

1451. In Romans 8, we have received a spirit of sonship with God that makes us cry out what?

1452. What does the Spirit testify to our spirit in Romans 8?

1453. And if we are God's children, then we are also what?

1454. Romans 8 says that for us to share in Christ's glory we must share in his what?

1455. Romans 8 says that our present sufferings are not worth comparing to our future what?

1456. In Romans 8, what has been subjected to frustration right up to the present time?

1457. In Romans 8, Paul wrote that creation has been groaning like the pains experienced during what?

1458. Who helps us with our weakness and intercedes for us according to Romans 8?

1459. What kind of wordless sounds is the Spirit making on our behalf?

1460. God works for the good of those who love him, who have been called according to his what?

1461. In Romans 8, what is Jesus doing for us at the right hand of God?

1462. In Romans 8, what are we more than through him who loved us?

1463. In Romans 8, of all the things that cannot separate us from the love of God, which two are measurements?

1464. In Romans 9, for whose sake did Paul wish he was cut off?

1465. In Romans 9, Paul said it is not those of physical descent who are God's children, but the children of what?

1466. In Romans 9, Paul said the potter has the right to make pottery for noble use and what other kind of use?

1467. According to Romans 9, what did the Israelites stumble over?

1468. In Romans 10, Paul expressed his heart's desire for who to be saved?

1469. In Romans 10, Paul testified that the Israelites had a zeal for God but it was not based on what?

1470. In Romans 10:9, what does it say we must declare with our mouth?

1471. According to Romans 10:9, what must we believe in our heart?

1472. According to Romans 10:10, with what do we believe and are justified?

1473. According to Romans 10:10, with what do we confess and are saved?

1474. According to Romans 10:13, what happens to everyone who calls on the name of the Lord?

1475. In Romans 10, Paul reminded us that it's beautiful when a person's feet bring what to others?

1476. In Romans 10, Paul reminded us that God has held out what to a disobedient and obstinate people?

1477. What tribe of Israel did Paul say he descended from?

1478. In Romans 11, Paul spoke of a remnant of believers just like in the time of what prophet?

1479. According to Romans 11, if we are saved by grace, then salvation is no longer based on what?

1480. In Romans 11, Paul said salvation came to the Gentiles to make whom jealous?

1481. When Paul spoke of grafting in branches in Romans 11, what kind of a tree did he use as an example?

1482. In this example, Paul said the branches are not superior to what because they don't support it?

1483. In Romans 11, Paul said Israel had experienced a hardening until a full number of what group came into the faith?

1484. What did Romans 12 say we should offer our bodies as?

1485. What did Romans 12 say we should not conform to any longer?

1486. How did Romans 12 say we can be transformed?

1487. Once we do that, what can we test and approve?

1488. In Christ, we are many who form one what?

1489. In Romans 12, Paul told the people to rejoice with those who were doing what?

1490. In Romans 12, Paul told the people not to take revenge but to leave room for what?

1491. In Romans 12, what two actions did Paul tell the people to do for their enemies when they were in need?

1492. In Romans 12, Paul told the people that by feeding their enemy, they would heap what on their heads?

1493. In Romans 12, Paul told the people to overcome evil with what?

1494. Who does Romans 13 say we should submit ourselves to?

1495. We must submit to governing authorities not only because of possible punishment, but because of what?

1496. What four things does Romans 13 say we should give God's governing authorities?

1497. We should put aside the deeds of darkness and put on the armor of what?

1498. What does Romans 13 tell us to clothe ourselves in?

1499. Romans 14 says one man's faith allows him to eat everything, but the one whose faith is weak eats only what food?

1500. Romans 14:17 says the kingdom of God is not a matter of what two things?

1501. What two things does Romans 14 say it is better not to do than to cause a brother to fail?

1502. Who did Paul feel needed to hear the Gospel because of promises made to the patriarchs?

1503. According to Romans 15, where did Paul prefer to preach the gospel?

1504. What European country did Paul say in Romans 15 that he planned to visit?

1505. What two Gentile regions made contributions for the poor in Jerusalem?

1506. In Romans 16, what role did Phoebe hold at the church?

1507. What couple did Paul thank in Romans 16 for risking their lives for him?

1508. Who does Paul say in Romans 16 was the first convert to Christ in the province of Asia?

1509. What two ways do divisive people deceive the minds of naïve people?

1510. Who did Paul say in Romans 16 would soon be crushed under their feet?

1511. Who was the person, with two books of the Bible named after him, that Paul mentioned during his final greetings in Romans?

1512. Who wrote down this entire letter to the Romans?

1513. Who was the city's director of public works mentioned in Romans 16?

1 Corinthians

1514. Who did Paul write 1 Corinthians with?

1515. As the church in Corinth waited for Jesus Christ to be revealed, what did Paul tell them not to lack?

1516. Whose household informed Paul that there were divisions in the Corinthian church?

1517. In 1 Corinthians 1, what four people did the people quarrel about and say they were followers of?

1518. What two people did Paul mention by name that he baptized?

1519. Whose household did Paul remember he baptized?

1520. Paul felt he was not sent to baptize but to do what?

1521. What did Paul say the Jews demanded for their faith?

1522. What did Paul say the Greeks always looked for?

1523. In 1 Corinthians 1, Paul said God chose the foolish and weak things of the world to shame what two groups of people?

1524. What did Paul say he did not use to convince the Corinthians with his testimony?

1525. Paul said he did not deliver his message to the Corinthians using what kind of words?

1526. In 1 Corinthians 2, whose mind did Paul say that they had?

1527. Because they were infants in Christ, Paul didn't feed them solid food, but what?

1528. In 1 Corinthians, Paul said he planted seeds but who watered them?

1529. Who made it all grow?

1530. According to Paul in 1 Corinthians 3, what is the foundation of a person's spiritual life?

1531. What six items will people try to build their foundation on instead?

1532. What will test the quality of each man's work?

1533. If God's spirit lives in us, then what structure of God's are we, according to Paul in 1 Corinthians 3?

1534. Who did Paul in 1 Corinthians 4 call cursed, weak, hungry, homeless, and the scum of the earth?

1535. Who did Paul send to the Corinthians to teach them?

1536. In 1 Corinthians 4, Paul said God's kingdom is about power and not about what?

1537. When Paul promised to visit the Corinthians, what weapon did he threaten to come with?

1538. In 1 Corinthians 5, Paul was upset that a man was sleeping with whose wife?

1539. In 1 Corinthians 5, to whom did Paul say the Corinthian church should hand over the sexually immoral man?

1540. In 1 Corinthians 5, Paul said not to associate with a brother or sister who committed what sin?

1541. In 1 Corinthians 6, who did Paul say that the Lord's people will judge one day?

1542. What place did Paul say brothers should not take each other right in front of unbelievers?

1543. In 1 Corinthians 6, our bodies are members of Christ and should not be united with whom?

1544. What kind of sin is different from others because it sins against a person's own body?

1545. According to 1 Corinthians 6, our bodies are temples for whom?

1546. In 1 Corinthians 7, what did Paul say it was good for a man not to do?

1547. Who are the only two people Paul said could have sexual relationships?

1548. What of a wife's is not hers, but belongs to her husband—and vice versa?

1549. What is the only reason a husband and wife could deprive each other of physical contact?

1550. The husband and wife need to unite sexually over time because satan will tempt them due to their lack of what?

1551. Paul said it's better to marry than to burn with what?

1552. In 1 Corinthians 7, Paul said circumcision and uncircumcision are nothing, but what really counts?

1553. In 1 Corinthians 7, a woman is bound to her husband in marriage until what happens?

1554. In 1 Corinthians 8, love builds up but what does knowledge do?

1555. In 1 Corinthians 8, Paul warned against the practice of eating food sacrificed to what?

1556. In 1 Corinthians 8, what food was Paul willing not to eat to keep his brothers from falling into sin?

1557. Besides some of the other apostles, who else did Paul say was married?

1558. Why did Paul become all things to all men?

1559. In 1 Corinthians 9, Paul said all runners run but only one gets what?

1560. In 1 Corinthians 9, what do runners run for that does not last, but a follower of Christ receives one that lasts forever?

1561. In chapter 9, who did Paul tell the Corinthians not to fight like, as one just beating the air?

1562. In 1 Corinthians 10, who did Paul say was the spiritual rock that all the Israelites and Moses drank from in the desert?

1563. 1 Corinthians 10 says God will not let us be tempted beyond what?

1564. In those temptation situations, what does God always provide?

1565. 1 Corinthians 10 says we cannot drink from the cup of the Lord and what other cup?

1566. In 1 Corinthians 10, Paul said everything is permissible but not everything is what?

1567. If someone gives you food offered to sacrifices, what did Paul say you should do?

1568. What three specific groups did Paul say we should not cause to stumble?

1569. In 1 Corinthians 11, Paul said every man who prays or prophesies with his head covered dishonors what?

1570. In 1 Corinthians 11, what kind of hair for a man was called a disgrace?

1571. Paul said every time they ate the bread and drank the cup, they proclaimed what until Jesus returns?

1572. 1 Corinthians 11 says a man ought to examine himself before he does what?

1573. In the list of spiritual gifts found in 1 Corinthians 12:8–10, which one came first?

1574. In the list of spiritual gifts found in 1 Corinthians 12:8–10, which one came last?

1575. In Paul's example about the body of Christ in 1 Corinthians 12, what part of the body does the foot believe it should be?

1576. In Paul's example about the body of Christ in 1 Corinthians 12, what part of the body does the ear believe it should be?

1577. What part of the body could the eye not reject and say it didn't need it?

1578. What part of the body could the head not reject and say it didn't need it?

1579. In the list of roles found in the church body, which one comes first?

1580. Which one is listed last?

1581. In 1 Corinthians 13, if someone speaks in tongues but has not love, what two things does he sound like?

1582. Of all the qualities of love listed in 1 Corinthians 13:4–8, which comes first?

1583. According to 1 Corinthians 13, what does love keep no record of?

1584. What three spiritual gifts will one day cease, be stilled, and pass away?

1585. Paul said we only see a reflection of God in this world now, but we will one day see him how?

1586. At the end of 1 Corinthians 13, Paul said three things remain. What are they?

1587. What is the greatest of these three?

1588. Of all the spiritual gifts, which one did Paul say we should eagerly desire in 1 Corinthians 14?

1589. When someone prophesies, who do they edify?

1590. How many intelligible words did Paul wish to speak compared to 10,000 words in a tongue?

1591. According to Paul in 1 Corinthians 14, who are tongues a sign for?

1592. A person speaking in tongues should keep quiet in church if there is no what?

1593. In 1 Corinthians 14, God is not a God of disorder but of what?

1594. What did Paul call a disgrace in 1 Corinthians 14?

1595. If a woman has a question in church, who should she ask when she gets home?

1596. Who did Paul say Jesus first appeared to in his account of the resurrection in 1 Corinthians 15?

1597. How many of the brothers and sisters in Christ did Jesus appear to after the resurrection according to Paul's account in 1 Corinthians 15?

1598. Some of those Jesus appeared to were living when Paul wrote this, but what had happened to the others since then?

1599. In 1 Corinthians 15, Paul said he did not deserve to be called what?

1600. Why did Paul believe he did not deserve to be called an apostle?

1601. What two things were useless, according to Paul in 1 Corinthians 15, if Christ had not been raised?

1602. 1 Corinthians 15 said death came through one man. Who was that?

1603. What is the last enemy to be destroyed according to 1 Corinthians 15?

1604. What did Paul say he fought in Ephesus in 1 Corinthians 15?

1605. In 1 Corinthians 15, what did Paul say corrupted good morals?

1606. In 1 Corinthians 15, Paul said man has a different flesh than what three other creatures?

1607. In 1 Corinthians 15:40, there's a difference between earthly bodies and what other kind of bodies?

1608. In 1 Corinthians 15, Paul said the body sown is perishable, but will be raised how?

1609. According to 1 Corinthians 15, the first man was of earth and the second man was of what?

1610. According to 1 Corinthians 15, what cannot inherit the kingdom of God?

1611. In 1 Corinthians 15, at the sound of what instrument will we all be changed?

1612. In 1 Corinthians 15, what will death be swallowed up in?

1613. What is the sting of death according to 1 Corinthians 15?

1614. What is the power of sin according to 1 Corinthians 15?

1615. Paul repeated instructions about offerings that he told to what other group of churches?

1616. What church did Paul need to visit first before arriving in Corinth?

1617. Which two men was Paul going to send to the church in Corinth?

1618. Whose household was the first to convert in Achaia according to Paul in 1 Corinthians 16?

1619. What husband and wife team sent their greetings to the church in Corinth?

1620. In 1 Corinthians 16, Paul told the readers to greet one another with a holy what?

2 Corinthians

1621. In 2 Corinthians, Paul mentioned the troubles he experienced in the province of what continent?

1622. Paul had hoped to visit Corinth on his way to what region?

1623. What did God put in our hearts as a deposit, guaranteeing what is to come, according to 2 Corinthians 1?

1624. In 2 Corinthians 2, Paul forgave so that who would not outwit hm?

1625. When Paul went to Troas, who did he hope to find there?

1626. In 2 Corinthians 3, Paul said the lives of believers are not written on tablets of stone but on what kind of tablets?

1627. Paul said that we are ministers of a new gospel of the spirit and not ministers of what?

1628. In 2 Corinthians 3, Paul compared the veil over the hearts of men to the veil that covered the face of what Old Testament person?

1629. In 2 Corinthians 4, what did Paul say we carry our treasure around in?

1630. In 2 Corinthians 4, what did Paul tell us to fix our eyes on?

1631. Paul contrasted our eternal house in heaven to an earthly what?

1632. The eternal house in heaven was not built by what?

1633. What has God given us as a deposit, guaranteeing what is to come?

1634. As long as we are home in the body, we are away from what?

1635. We live by faith and not by what, according to 2 Corinthians 5?

1636. Paul preferred to be away from the body and where instead?

1637. If anyone is in Christ, he is a new what?

1638. According to 2 Corinthians 5, God gave Christians a ministry and a message of what?

1639. God made him who knew no sin to be sin so that we could know what?

1640. In 2 Corinthians 6, what did Paul tell the church not to put in anyone's path?

1641. Who did Paul tell believers not be yoked together with?

1642. Who was the representative sent to the Corinthians that encouraged Paul in 2 Corinthians 7 and 8?

1643. What did Paul realize caused the Corinthians deep sorrow?

1644. In 2 Corinthians 7, Paul was happy that his previous letter hurt the church because it led them to what?

1645. Where was the group of churches from that gave to Paul's cause out of their overflowing joy and extreme poverty?

1646. Paul said in 2 Corinthians 8 that Jesus Christ was rich but for our sake became what?

1647. What two actions in 2 Corinthians 9 did Paul say will produce results sparingly or generously?

1648. What kind of a giver does God love in 2 Corinthians 9?

1649. What did Paul say we need to take captive and make obedient to Christ?

1650. What did Paul say he didn't want to frighten the Corinthians with?

1651. If people were to boast, Paul said, they should boast in whom?

1652. In 2 Corinthians 11, what three "different" messages did Paul warn the church not to receive from other people?

1653. What church supplied Paul with what he needed?

1654. What does satan masquerade himself as?

1655. What punishment did Paul receive five times?

1656. How many lashes did Paul receive each time?

1657. How many times was Paul beaten with rods?

1658. How many times was Paul shipwrecked?

1659. Paul said he boasts of things that show his what?

1660. In the city of the Damascenes, how was Paul lowered over the wall?

1661. Paul said he knew a man who, fourteen years ago, was caught up into what?

1662. What did God give Paul to keep him from becoming conceited?

1663. Who sent this message of the thorn?

1664. How many times did Paul plead for the thorn in the flesh to be removed?

1665. What did God say was sufficient for Paul during this time?

1666. How did God make his power perfect in people?

1667. According to Paul in 2 Corinthians 12, what three things demonstrated the mark of a true apostle?

1668. According to 2 Corinthians, how many times had Paul visited Corinth?

1669. In 2 Corinthians 12, why was Paul afraid to visit the church again?

1670. With what kind of kiss did Paul ask people to greet one another?

Galatians

1671. What heavenly being did Paul say the people should not listen to if it preached a different gospel?

1672. In Galatians 1, who was Paul not trying to win the approval of?

1673. Before Paul converted, what cause was he trying to advance?

1674. After Paul's conversion, where did he go first before meeting the apostles?

1675. After how many years in Damascus did Paul then go to Jerusalem?

1676. How many days did Paul get acquainted with Peter after arriving in Jerusalem?

1677. Besides Peter, Paul only saw one other apostle. Who was it?

1678. When Paul went to Jerusalem, what two people did he take with him?

1679. Who was the Greek companion of Paul's that went to Jerusalem but did not feel compelled to be circumcised?

1680. In Galatians 2, Paul was called to the Gentiles as who felt called to the Jews?

1681. Name the three pillars mentioned in Galatians 2 who accepted Paul's ministry to Gentiles.

1682. Who did Paul oppose over the matter of associating with Gentiles?

1683. Where did Paul oppose him?

1684. Which apostle pulled away from the Gentiles when certain men came to town?

1685. What companion of Paul was led astray by the hypocrisy of the circumcision group in Galatians 2?

1686. Galatians 2:19 says we died to what so that we might live for God?

1687. What cannot be gained through the law, or Christ died for nothing?

1688. In Galatians 3, what do people have that make them children of Abraham?

1689. In Galatians 3:12, what is the law not based on?

1690. According to Galatians 3:13 (and Deuteronomy 21:23), cursed is everyone who hangs on a what?

1691. How many years after Abraham, according to Paul in Galatians 3, did Moses receive the law?

1692. Before faith in Christ came, what does Galatians 3 say we were held prisoners by?

1693. Besides Jew and Gentile, slave and free, who else did Paul say in Galatians 3 was one in Christ Jesus?

1694. Since we are no longer a slave, but a son, then what are we ultimately?

1695. What was the reason Paul said that first led him to preach the gospel to the Galatians?

1696. What man's two sons did Paul compare to the struggle of the law of slavery versus the promise of freedom?

1697. Which mother did Paul say in Galatians 4 represented Mount Sinai?

1698. In Galatians 4, Paul said believers are not children of the slave woman but of what kind of woman?

1699. Paul said in Galatians 5 that if people get circumcised, who will be of no value to them?

1700. Paul said everyone who got circumcised was obligated to the whole what?

1701. In Paul's metaphor from Galatians 5, what works its way through a whole batch of dough?

1702. Paul said in Galatians 5 that those who engage in the acts of the flesh do not inherit what?

1703. Name the fruits of the Spirit from Galatians 5 in order.

1704. If someone was caught in sin, how should a spiritual person restore him?

1705. Paul said in Galatians 6 that we should carry each other's what?

1706. Paul said we should not grow weary doing what?

1707. Toward whom should we especially do the most good?

1708. What kind of letters did Paul write with his own hand at the end of Galatians?

1709. In Galatians 6, Paul said not to boast about ourselves, but what instead?

1710. What did Paul say at the end of Galatians that he bore on his body?

Ephesians

1711. According to Ephesians 1, what two qualities did God choose us to be in his sight?

1712. In Ephesians 1, what did God predestine us for, in love, through Jesus Christ?

1713. What are believers marked with according to Ephesians 1?

1714. Who is that seal?

1715. According to Ephesians 1, the Holy Spirit is a deposit guaranteeing our what?

1716. Where did God place all things under Jesus?

1717. What did God appoint Jesus to be head over?

1718. According to Ephesians 2, God made us alive in Christ even when we were dead in our what?

1719. By what have we been saved?

1720. According to Ephesians 2, since grace is not by works, what can we not do?

1721. According to Ephesians 2, we were created in Christ Jesus to do what?

1722. According to Ephesians 2, what has brought the outsiders (Gentiles, uncircumcised) near?

1723. According to Ephesians 2, what did Christ preach to those far away and near?

1724. As a result, we are all fellow citizens with God's people and no longer what?

1725. God's household was built on the foundation of what two groups of people?

1726. What chief part of the building was Christ Jesus?

1727. To what people group was the "mystery" of the gospel made known according to Ephesians 3?

1728. In Ephesians 3, how can we now approach God through faith?

1729. What, in Ephesians 3, is wide and long, high and deep?

1730. According to Ephesians 3, how much more is God able to do than we could ever ask or imagine?

1731. Name the "ones" mentioned in Ephesians 4:4-5. Hint: there are seven.

1732. In Ephesians 4, Paul said we will no longer be like infants, tossed around by what?

1733. Who is the head of the mature body (of believers) according to Paul in Ephesians 4?

1734. In Ephesians 4, who should a Christian no longer live like in the futility of their thinking?

1735. In Ephesians 4, Paul said to put off the old _____ and put on the new _____.

1736. What should a Christian not let the sun go down on?

1737. By not reconciling our anger, according to Paul in Ephesians 4, who gets a foothold?

1738. In Ephesians 4, what kind of "talk" did Paul say should not come from a believer's mouth?

1739. Ephesians 4 tells us not to grieve who?

1740. In Ephesians 5, instead of obscenity, foolish talk, and coarse joking coming from our mouths, there should be what?

1741. In Ephesians 5, Paul said to make the most of every opportunity because he described the days as what?

1742. Instead of getting drunk on wine, Ephesians 5 said we should be filled with what?

1743. In Ephesians 5, the husband is the head of the wife as Christ is the head of what?

1744. In Ephesians 5, husbands ought to love their wives as much as they love what?

1745. What will the two become when a man leaves his parents and becomes united to his wife?

1746. In Ephesians 5, the husband must love his wife and what must the wife show her husband?

1747. Which commandment mentioned in Ephesians 6 comes with a promise?

1748. Who should fathers not exasperate according to Ephesians 6?

1749. Whose schemes does the armor of God protect you against?

1750. According to Ephesians 6, what is our struggle not against?

1751. Which piece of the armor of God was buckled around the waist?

1752. What piece of the armor of God was described as righteousness?

1753. Our feet, fitted with readiness, came from the gospel of what?

1754. What did the shield of faith extinguish?

1755. What part of faith did the helmet represent?

1756. What was the sword of the spirit also known as?

1757. In Ephesians 6, Paul described himself as an ambassador wearing what?

1758. In the closing statement from Ephesians, what dear brother did Paul send to Ephesus to encourage them?

Philippians

1759. What two people addressed the Philippians in the opening line of the letter?

1760. Paul was confident that God's good work through the Philippians would be carried on to completion until what day?

1761. To whom in the palace was it clear that Paul was in chains for Christ?

1762. In Philippians 1, who became more confident and bold because of Paul's chains?

1763. According to Philippians 1, from what three motivations do people preach the gospel?

1764. Despite false motives, what was the most important thing according to Paul in Philippians 1?

1765. For Paul, to live is Christ and what is gain?

1766. In Philippians 1, Paul said the people would not only believe in Christ, but it would be granted that they would also do what for him?

1767. What did Paul say we should do nothing out of?

1768. According to Philippians 2, who should we have the same mindset as?

1769. In Philippians 2, Jesus took the very nature of a what?

1770. In Philippians 2, Jesus took the appearance of what?

1771. Jesus was obedient all the way to what point?

1772. At the very name of Jesus, every what will bow?

1773. In what three places will they bow?

1774. What will every tongue confess?

1775. In Philippians 2, Paul told the readers to work out their salvation with what?

1776. In Philippians 2, Paul said if the church were blameless and pure, they would shine like what?

1777. Paul, in Philippians 2, mentioned being poured out like a what?

1778. Who did Paul hope to send to the church in Philippi?

1779. Who did Paul say in Philippians 2 he was sending to the church and also delivered the letter?

1780. What almost happened to Epaphroditus?

1781. What tribe did Paul say he was from?

1782. What Jewish religious title did Paul hold?

1783. How did Paul describe every title and gain in his life since meeting Christ?

1784. Paul said in Philippians 3 that he wanted to know Christ and the power of His what?

1785. In Philippians 3, Paul said he pressed on toward the _____ to win the _____ for which God called him heavenward.

1786. In Philippians 3, Paul spoke of the enemies of the cross and said their god was their what?

1787. What kind of "things" were the minds of God's enemies set on, according to Paul in Philippians 3?

1788. In Philippians 3, where did Paul say his citizenship was?

1789. What two women did Paul plead with to be of the same mind in Philippians 4?

1790. What does Philippians 4:4 say we should do always?

1791. In order not to be anxious, what three steps did Paul say we needed to take, according to Philippians 4:6?

1792. According to Philippians 4:7, what will guard our hearts and minds?

1793. In Philippians 4:11, what had Paul learned to be in any circumstance?

1794. In Philippians 4:13, Paul said he could do all things through God who gave him what?

1795. Where was Paul heading when the church in Philippi sent him a gift?

1796. Whose household sent a greeting to the church in Philippi?

Colossians

1797. Who did Paul write Colossians with?

1798. What did Paul say was bearing fruit and growing throughout the whole world?

1799. Who was the faithful minister that served with the Colossians?

1800. Paul said that God had rescued his people from the dominion of what?

1801. Colossians 1 said Jesus was the firstborn over all what?

1802. Jesus is the head of the body, which goes by what other name?

1803. Through what did Jesus make peace?

1804. No longer are we alienated, Paul said in Colossians 1, but because of Jesus' body, we are now what?

1805. According to Paul in this chapter, to whom has the mystery of Christ now been revealed?

1806. In Colossians 2, Paul said he struggled for those in Colosse and what other city?

1807. In Colossians 2, Paul said he was absent from the congregation in body but not absent in what other way?

1808. How did Paul describe the philosophy that has taken many captive?

1809. In Colossians 2, Paul said those deceptive philosophies depended on what two things and not on Christ?

1810. In Colossians 2, Jesus nailed our legal indebtedness to what?

1811. In Colossians 3, what did Paul say should rule in their hearts?

1812. In Colossians 3, what three things did Paul say we should teach and admonish one another with?

1813. What did Paul tell wives to do to their husbands?

1814. What did Paul tell husbands to do to their wives?

1815. What did Paul tell children to do to their parents?

1816. Who did Paul tell fathers not to embitter?

1817. In Colossians 3, Paul said slaves should work for their masters as if working for whom?

1818. In Colossians 4, what seasoning did Paul say all conversations should have?

1819. Who did Paul mention in Colossians 4 that he was sending to them to give them an update about Paul's circumstances?

1820. Who did Paul send to the Colossians that was also mentioned in the book of Philemon?

1821. Who was Paul's fellow prisoner mentioned in Colossians 4?

1822. Name the cousin of Barnabas whom Paul mentioned in Colossians 4.

1823. Who was the doctor Paul mentioned?

1824. What city did Paul mention in Colossians 4 that was also a city mentioned in Revelation 3?

1825. When Paul wrapped up his letter to the Colossians, what did he tell them to remember?

1 Thessalonians

1826. Paul and what two other people wrote 1 Thessalonians?

1827. In 1 Thessalonians, Paul applauded the church because it became a model to all the believers in what two regions?

1828. In 1 Thessalonians 2, Paul said that before they visited Thessalonica, they had suffered and been treated outrageously in what city?

1829. Who did Paul say in 1 Thessalonians 2 that they were not trying to please?

1830. Who did Paul blame in 1 Thessalonians 2 for blocking his arrival over and over to the church?

1831. In what city did Paul say they thought it was best to be left by themselves?

1832. Who did Paul send to Thessalonica to strengthen and encourage their faith?

1833. What did Paul not want the people to be uninformed about in 1 Thessalonians 4?

1834. What did Paul not want people to grieve without?

1835. The sound of what instrument will precede the dead rising?

1836. Who will rise first at the coming of the Lord?

1837. Who will be last to catch up with the Lord in the air?

1838. What will the day of the Lord come like, as described in 1 Thessalonians 5?

1839. In 1 Thessalonians 5, Paul said the church should not be like people of the night, but people of what?

1840. What two pieces of the armor of God, mentioned in Ephesians, did Paul refer to in 1 Thessalonians 5?

1841. What did Paul tell the people not to quench in 1 Thessalonians 5?

1842. What did Paul tell the people not to treat with contempt?

2 Thessalonians

1843. Both letters to Thessalonica are from the same three people. Who are they?

1844. In 2 Thessalonians, Paul wanted to correct any false teaching that said what day had come?

1845. The man of lawlessness, whom Paul predicted would come, sets himself up in what holy place?

1846. What kind of "counterfeit" works will the lawless one display, according to 2 Thessalonians 2?

1847. In 2 Thessalonians 2, Paul said those that perish do so because they refused to love what?

1848. What two ways did Paul say that the church received his teachings?

1849. In 2 Thessalonians 3, what did Paul do day and night when he was with them so he would not be a burden on them?

1850. Paul said, "The one who is unwilling to work shall not _____."

1851. Paul said some in the church were not busy but busy _____.

NEW TESTAMENT
Challenge

1 Timothy

1852. Where was Timothy when Paul wrote to him in 1 Timothy?

1853. What did Paul say in 1 Timothy 1 that he was the worst of?

1854. What two people did Paul mention by name that had shipwrecked their faith?

1855. Who did Paul hand these two over to so they could be taught not to blaspheme?

1856. Who did Paul say they needed to pray for in 1 Timothy 2 so that they lead peaceful and quiet lives?

1857. What did Paul want all men to lift in prayer?

1858. How did Paul want women to dress?

1859. What non-material thing did Paul want women to adorn themselves with?

1860. What two positions in the church did Paul give character evaluations for in 1 Timothy 3?

1861. What must an overseer manage well before he can manage God's church?

1862. To be an overseer, what must not have recently occurred in his life?

1863. To be an overseer, who must he also have a good reputation with?

1864. What must a deacon not indulge much in?

1865. In 1 Timothy 4, Paul warned Timothy that some in later times would follow deceiving spirits and teach things taught by what?

1866. In 1 Timothy 4, Paul warned Timothy that some teaching forbid people to marry and to abstain from certain kinds of what?

1867. Paul told Timothy not to let anyone look down on him just because he was what?

1868. If someone did not provide for their family, what were they worse than?

1869. How old did a widow need to be in order to receive care from the church, according to 1 Timothy 5?

1870. According to 1 Timothy 5, what did younger widows have the habit of becoming?

1871. If accusations arose against an elder, how many witnesses must come forward?

1872. What did 1 Timothy 5 say a person should drink a little of in addition to water to help with one's stomach and illnesses?

1873. In 1 Timothy 6, an unhealthy interest over what caused controversies and quarrels?

1874. What did some think was a means to financial gain?

1875. What two things did Paul feel we should be content having?

1876. The love of money is the root of all kinds of what?

1877. When eager for money, what have some pierced themselves with to get it?

1878. In 1 Timothy 6, Paul told Timothy to fight the good fight of what?

1879. In 1 Timothy 6, Paul referenced Jesus' good confession to whom?

1880. Instead of money, what does Paul say we should be rich in?

1881. Many have departed from the faith because of godless chatter they falsely called what?

2 Timothy

1882. Who was Timothy's grandmother?

1883. Who was Timothy's mother?

1884. In 2 Timothy 1, Paul said the Spirit does not make us what, but gives us power, love, and self-discipline?

1885. Paul mentioned two people in 2 Timothy 1, Phygelus and Hermogenes. What did they do to him?

1886. Whose household did Paul ask the Lord to show mercy to because they refreshed Paul on many occasions?

1887. Paul asked that Timothy present himself as a workman who correctly handled what?

1888. Paul said that false teaching spread like what kind of sickness?

1889. What did false teachers like Hymenaeus and Philetus say had already taken place?

1890. What do foolish and stupid arguments only lead to?

1891. What Old Testament figure did Jannes and Jambres oppose according to 2 Timothy 3?

1892. In 2 Timothy 3, name the three places Paul mentioned where he faced persecution.

1893. According to 2 Timothy 3, all Scripture is useful for what four things?

1894. According to 2 Timothy 3, what does Scripture equip a servant to do?

1895. What did Paul fear one day people would not put up with?

1896. In order to hear what they want to hear, what itching part of the body will people satisfy to suit their own desires?

1897. Paul said people will turn away from truth and turn to what?

1898. What was Paul being poured out like?

1899. In 2 Timothy 4, Paul said he fought the good what?

1900. What did he finish while keeping the faith?

1901. What kind of crown did Paul long to be awarded?

1902. Who deserted Paul and went to Thessalonica?

1903. While Paul wrote 2 Timothy, who was the only person with him at the time?

1904. Who did Paul mention in 2 Timothy 4 that he wanted Timothy to bring next time because he was so helpful to the ministry?

1905. What two items did Paul forget on his last trip that he wanted brought to him?

1906. What was the name of the metalworker who did Paul a great deal of harm?

1907. What husband and wife team did Paul send his greetings to?

Titus

1908. On what island did Paul leave Titus?

1909. Who did Paul want Titus to appoint in every town?

1910. In Titus 1, what group did Paul call rebellious, talkers, and deceivers?

1911. According to Paul in the book of Titus, who were always called liars, evil brutes, and lazy gluttons?

1912. In Titus 1, Paul said people claim to know God, but what denies that they really do?

1913. What group of men did Paul tell Titus to teach to be temperate, worthy of respect, self-controlled?

1914. What group of women did Paul tell Titus to teach to be reverent, not slanderers, and examples to younger women?

1915. In the book of Titus, what should older women not be addicted to?

1916. What group of women did Paul say needed to be self-controlled, pure, busy at home, and kind?

1917. What group of men did Paul tell Titus to encourage to be self-controlled and to set an example to them by doing good?

1918. What group did Paul tell Titus to teach to be subject to their masters and not to talk back?

1919. According to Titus 3, we are saved by the washing of rebirth and renewal from whom?

1920. According to the book of Titus, how many times should a divisive person be warned before you have nothing to do with them?

1921. Where did Paul, at the end of Titus, say he wanted to winter?

1922. What profession was Paul's friend Zenas?

Philemon

1923. Who wrote the letter of Philemon with Paul?

1924. Who were the other two people Paul addressed the letter of Philemon to?

1925. What condition was Paul in when Onesimus became his son?

1926. Paul said Onesimus was no longer a slave but a what?

1927. What did Paul offer to do about any damages Onesimus had caused?

1928. What did Paul remind Philemon that he owed him?

1929. What did Paul ask Philemon to prepare for him?

1930. Who was also a prisoner with Paul that sent his greetings?

1931. In Philemon, Paul extended greetings from what two people who have the same names as two Gospels?

Hebrews

1932. Who is the radiance of God's glory and the exact representation of his being?

1933. Hebrews 1 says Christ is superior over what other heavenly beings?

1934. What will one day wear out like a garment, roll up like a robe, and one day be changed?

1935. Who was Jesus made lower than for a little while?

1936. Who holds the power of death according to Hebrews 2?

1937. Hebrews 3 says Christ is faithful as a son over God's house, but what Old Testament person was faithful as a servant in God's house?

1938. What does Hebrews 3 ask brothers and sisters to do daily to each other so none can be hardened by sin's deceitfulness?

1939. What is the word of God sharper than, according to Hebrews 4?

1940. What four things does the word of God penetrate and divide?

1941. Hebrews says we have a high priest who is able to sympathize with our what?

1942. Hebrews 4:15 says Jesus was tempted but he did not what?

1943. By whose priestly "order" was Jesus designated to be high priest?

1944. Speaking to the spiritual maturity of the readers, the writer of Hebrews said the people needed milk and not what?

1945. When God made a promise to Abraham, according to Hebrews 6, who did he swear by?

1946. According to Hebrews 6, what is it impossible for God to do?

1947. Who was the priest/king of Salem the writer compared Jesus to in Hebrews 7?

1948. What does *Melchizedek* mean?

1949. What does the *king of Salem* mean?

1950. According to Hebrews 7, what four things about Melchizedek were unknown?

1951. What descendants did Melchizedek not trace his lineage to even though he performed their duties?

1952. According to Hebrews 7, the Melchizedek priesthood was not like what other priesthood?

1953. Jesus descended from what tribe, which had nothing to do with the priesthood?

1954. According to Hebrews 8, what here on earth is a copy and a shadow of what is in heaven?

1955. What did Jesus offer that was new and superior, because God found the old obsolete?

1956. According to Hebrews 9, what items were inside the ark of the covenant?

1957. According to Hebrews 9, What room did the high priest enter once a year?

1958. According to Hebrews 9, Jesus did not enter the tabernacle by means of the blood of what two animals?

1959. God required by the law that everything be cleansed with what?

1960. According to Hebrews 9, without the shedding of blood, there can be no what?

1961. How many times is man destined to die?

1962. According to Hebrews 10, what was only a shadow of the good things to come?

1963. According to Hebrews 10, what was impossible for the blood of bulls and goats to take away?

1964. According to Hebrews 10, what should believers not give up doing as some are in the habit of doing?

1965. Faith is being certain of what we do not _____.

1966. Who in Hebrews 11 did not experience death?

1967. According to Hebrews 11, without what is it impossible to please God?

1968. According to Hebrews 11, what two things must anyone who comes to God believe by faith?

1969. According to Hebrews 11, Abraham lived in tents, but he was looking forward to what?

1970. Who is the first woman mentioned in the Hebrews 11 list of the faithful?

1971. According to Hebrews 11, What kind of country were all these people looking forward to?

1972. In Hebrews 11, who did Moses refuse to be known as the son of?

1973. Name four people from the book of Judges whose faith is highlighted in Hebrews 11.

1974. Who was the only king mentioned in the list of the faithful from Hebrews 11?

1975. What are we surrounded by, according to Hebrews 12?

1976. If we endure hardship as discipline, then what is God treating us like?

1977. According to Hebrews 12, what does not seem pleasant at the time but later produces a harvest of righteousness?

1978. According to Hebrews 12, what are we receiving that cannot be shaken?

1979. By entertaining strangers, according to Hebrews 13, who may we be entertaining without knowing it?

1980. What should be kept pure in marriage according to Hebrews 13?

1981. Who is the same yesterday, today, and forever?

1982. Who was mentioned at the end of Hebrews that was a frequent companion of Paul?

1983. The author of Hebrews sent greetings from what country?

James

1984. To whom did James write this letter?

1985. According to James, when should believers consider it pure joy?

1986. According to James 1, what does the testing of our faith produce?

1987. What should you ask for if you realize you lack it?

1988. James said anyone who doubts is like what natural occurrence in the sea?

1989. Who did James in chapter 1 compare to a flower scorched by the heat and withering away?

1990. What reward will those who persevere under trial receive as promised by the Lord?

1991. Who cannot be tempted nor tempts, according to James 1?

1992. What should believers, according to James 1, be quick to do?

1993. What two things should believers be slow to do?

1994. What did James say is planted in us that can save us?

1995. James 1 says someone who listens to the word and doesn't do what it says is like someone who looks into a what and forgets what they look like?

1996. A pure and faultless religion, according to James 1, is the kind that looks after which two groups of people?

1997. When warning against favoritism, what did James say someone could offer a rich person but deny a poor person during a meeting?

1998. What does James 2 say the poor are rich in?

1999. What does James 2 say triumphs over judgment?

2000. What, according to James, without action, is dead?

2001. Who in James 2 believes there is one God and shudders?

2002. The faith of what two Old Testament people did James mention in chapter 2 when talking about faith accompanied by actions?

2003. What position in the church is judged more strictly according to James 3?

2004. James compared a bit in the mouth of what animal to the taming of the tongue?

2005. James compared what part of a ship to the taming of the tongue?

2006. James said the tongue was a like a small spark that could set what piece of property on fire?

2007. According to James 3, what can a person do to all kinds of animals but not to the human tongue?

2008. James wrote in chapter 3 that the tongue is evil, full of deadly what?

2009. James said the tongue cannot praise and curse just like a spring cannot produce what two types of water?

2010. James in chapter 4 said the people do not have because they do not what?

2011. We ask and do not receive because we ask with the wrong what?

2012. James said that if we are friends with what, then we are an enemy of God?

2013. Who must we resist and cause him to flee from us, according to James 4?

2014. James mentioned the perseverance of what Old Testament character in chapter 5?

2015. What did James say that the elders should anoint a sick person with?

2016. The prayer of what kind of person is powerful and effective according to James 5?

2017. What Old Testament rain-stopper did James mention in chapter 5?

1 Peter

2018. According to 1 Peter 1, where is our inheritance kept that can never perish, spoil, or fade?

2019. According to 1 Peter 1, what is the end result of our faith?

2020. In 1 Peter 1, why did Peter say we need to be holy?

2021. According to 1 Peter 1, what kind of perishable things are we not redeemed by?

2022. In 1 Peter 2, new believers, like newborn babies, should crave what kind of milk?

2023. In 1 Peter 2, Peter called believers living _____, being built up into a spiritual house.

2024. In 1 Peter 2, Peter said we, the chosen people, are a royal _____.

2025. What did Peter hope that pagans would see coming from believers and as a result glorify God?

2026. What does 1 Peter 2 say they hurled at Jesus but he did not retaliate?

2027. First Peter 2:24 quotes Isaiah, saying Jesus bore our sins and by his _____ we are healed.

2028. What kind of spirit reflects unfading beauty in a woman, according to 1 Peter 3:4?

2029. According to 1 Peter 3, how did the women of the past make themselves beautiful?

2030. Which Old Testament woman did Peter use as an example of this kind of submission?

2031. According to 1 Peter 3:15, we must always be prepared to give the reason for the _____ that we have.

2032. According to 1 Peter 3, where did Jesus preach to the spirits after being made alive?

2033. These spirits were around during the time of which Old Testament character?

2034. In 1 Peter 3, Peter said that the waters of Noah's time represented what Christian practice today?

2035. According to 1 Peter 4, what covers a multitude of sins?

2036. In 1 Peter 4, Peter said one should not be ashamed to suffer as a what?

2037. When the Chief Shepherd appears, what unfading crown will the faithful receive according to 1 Peter 5?

2038. In 1 Peter 5, what can we cast on him because he cares for us?

2039. What prowling animal did Peter compare the devil to?

2040. What two fellow workers did Peter mention that Paul wrote about frequently?

2 Peter

2041. In 2 Peter 1, where did Peter say he was when he heard God's voice speak about Jesus?

2042. No Scripture, according to 2 Peter 1, came about because of the prophet's own what?

2043. In 2 Peter 2, who did Peter describe as a preacher of righteousness?

2044. In 2 Peter 2, who was the righteous man living among lawless men that God rescued?

2045. Who was the beast without speech, mentioned in 2 Peter 2, who spoke with a man's voice and restrained a prophet's madness?

2046. What did false teachers, called slaves to depravity, promise their followers?

2047. How many years are like one day to the Lord?

2048. In 2 Peter 3, God does not want people to perish, but to come to what?

2049. The day of the Lord will come like what kind of criminal?

2050. What kind of lives should we live as we look forward to the day of the Lord?

2051. Whose letters did Peter reference as Scripture?

1 John

2052. In 1 John 1, with what three senses did the writer experience the Word of life firsthand?

2053. In 1 John 1, the writer said he wrote this letter to make what complete?

2054. God is light and in him is no what?

2055. If we walk in the light, then what do we have with another?

2056. If we confess our sins, he is faithful and just to do what two things?

2057. If we say we do not sin, what did the writer of 1 John say we make God out to be?

2058. The writer of 1 John says that we know him if we keep what?

2059. If you hate your brother, according to 1 John 2, what are you walking around in?

2060. What three things mentioned in 1 John 2 are from the world and do not come from the Father?

2061. Who did John warn was coming and many of them had already arrived?

2062. What does an antichrist deny?

2063. According to 1 John 3, who has been sinning since the beginning?

2064. Whose work did the Son of God want to destroy?

2065. As followers of Christ, we should not be surprised, said the writer of 1 John, if what hates us?

2066. According to 1 John 3, if you hate your brother or sister, what should you be called?

2067. According to 1 John 3, what did Jesus Christ do that showed true love?

2068. In 1 John 3, John said we should not love with words or tongue but with what?

2069. What should we test, according to 1 John 4, to see whether they are from God?

2070. What does every spirit from God acknowledge?

2071. According to 1 John 4, greater is the one in us than the one who is where?

2072. In 1 John 4, how did God show his love among us?

2073. What does perfect love drive out?

2074. According to 1 John 4, what does fear have to do with?

2075. We love because who first loved us?

2076. According to 1 John 4, if you love God and hate your brother or sister, what are you?

2077. 1 John 5 said in order to show God your love, you must be carrying out what?

2078. According to 1 John 5, what two liquids did Jesus come to us by?

2079. In 1 John 5, what three things testify to the truth about Jesus?

2080. According to 1 John 5, everyone who has the Son has what?

2081. 1 John ends with the writer telling the children to keep away from what?

2 John

2082. How did the writer of 2 John introduce himself in the letter?

2083. Who was 2 John addressed to?

2084. What do the deceivers and antichrists not acknowledge in their teachings?

2085. In 2 John, the writer said he had much to say but he didn't want to use what means to communicate?

2086. What did he prefer to do instead?

3 John

2087. Who did the writer of 3 John address himself as?

2088. To whom was 3 John written?

2089. Who was the troublemaker in the church that John pointed out in 3 John?

2090. What believer, mentioned in 3 John, was spoken well of by everyone?

2091. The writer of 3 John said he had much to write about but he didn't want to use what two things?

Jude

2092. Who did Jude indicate was his brother?

2093. According to Jude, who had slipped in among the people?

2094. Where are the angels who have abandoned God now kept?

2095. What famous twin cities were mentioned in Jude?

2096. Who was the archangel that disputed with the devil?

2097. Whose body was the dispute over?

2098. Jude compared the sins of the people to what three notorious Old Testament characters?

2099. What person, seventh in Adam's line, did Jude quote?

2100. Jude told readers to save people by snatching them from what?

Revelation

2101. What did God send John to make known the revelation?

2102. How many churches did John address in Revelation 1?

2103. On what continent were the churches located found in Revelation?

2104. John quoted in Revelation that every eye will see him, even those who did what?

2105. The Lord God said he is the Alpha and the what?

2106. On what island was John when he received the Revelation?

2107. How many lampstands did John see in Revelation 1?

2108. Standing amongst those lampstands was someone like whom?

2109. In Revelation 1, John compared the white hair of the Son of Man to what fabric?

2110. The man in John's vision had feet like bronze, glowing in a what?

2111. How many stars did John see in the hand of the Son of Man in Revelation 1?

2112. What was coming out of the mouth of the Son of Man in Revelation 1?

2113. In Revelation 1, the Son of Man told John he holds the keys to what two things?

2114. What were the seven stars, according to the Son of Man in Revelation 1?

2115. What were the seven lampstands, according to the Son of Man in Revelation 1?

2116. How many stars were in the hand of the one who spoke the words in Revelation 2?

2117. In what hand were the seven stars held?

2118. How many lampstands did the one who spoke the words walk amongst in Revelation 2?

2119. Who did the church of Ephesus not tolerate?

2120. Who did some claim to be but the church at Ephesus tested them?

2121. What did the church of Ephesus forsake?

2122. What did Jesus threaten to remove from them?

2123. In Revelation 2, what group's practices did the church of Ephesus hate?

2124. From what tree did God promise people would eat if they were victorious?

2125. Which church had afflictions and poverty but was rich?

2126. In Revelation 2, from what synagogue were those who slandered and said they were Jews?

2127. How many days of persecution did Jesus say the church of Smyrna would suffer?

2128. In Revelation 2, who had a throne in Pergamum?

2129. Who was the faithful witness put to death in Pergamum?

2130. What two teachings crept into the church of Pergamum?

2131. What color stone did Jesus promise those who are victorious?

2132. Who was the self-proclaimed prophetess that the church in Thyatira tolerated?

2133. What two things did she lead others to do?

2134. Jesus told the church in Sardis they had a reputation for being what?

2135. In Revelation 3, Jesus told the church in Sardis to wake up because he would come like a what?

2136. Jesus said there were few people in Sardis who had not soiled what?

2137. The one who brought the words to the church of Philadelphia held the key of what famous Jewish king?

2138. What did Jesus place before the church in Philadelphia that no one could shut?

2139. Whose synagogue was in Philadelphia, according to Revelation 3?

2140. What did Jesus tell the church of Philadelphia to hold to so no one would take it?

2141. Where will those who overcome become pillars, according to Jesus in Revelation 3?

2142. The church in Laodicea was neither one of what two temperatures?

2143. What temperature was the church in Laodicea?

2144. What did Jesus tell the church of Laodicea to put in their eyes?

2145. If someone opened the door, what did Jesus promise to come inside and do?

2146. What musical instrument did the voice from heaven speak like?

2147. What colorfully encircled the throne John saw in Revelation 4?

2148. How many other thrones encircled God's throne?

2149. Who were seated on those thrones?

2150. What was on their heads?

2151. How many lamps were blazing in front of the throne?

2152. What were those lamps?

2153. How many living creatures were there?

2154. What were the living creatures in Revelation 4 covered with?

2155. What four things did the four living creatures look like?

2156. What did each living creature in Revelation 4 have six of?

2157. What did the elders lay down before the throne in Revelation 4?

2158. How many seals sealed the scroll in Revelation 5?

2159. The one who took the scroll was described by three names in Revelation 5. What were they?

2160. How many horns and eyes did the Lamb have in Revelation 5?

2161. What two things were the four living creatures and the twenty-four elders holding in Revelation 5?

2162. What did the golden bowls of incense represent in Revelation 5?

2163. What did John see in Revelation 5 that numbered thousands upon thousands, ten thousand times ten thousand?

2164. What was the order by color of the horses that appeared with the breaking of the first four seals?

2165. What weapon was the rider of the white horse carrying?

2166. What weapon was the rider of the red horse given?

2167. What was the rider of the black horse in Revelation 6 carrying in his hands?

2168. Who was riding the pale horse?

2169. Who followed close behind the pale horse?

2170. In Revelation 6, by what four methods was death given the power to kill?

2171. What color robes were the souls given after the breaking of the fifth seal?

2172. At the breaking of the sixth seal, what color did the sun turn?

2173. What color did the moon turn?

2174. What four celestial bodies were affected after the breaking of the sixth seal?

2175. Where did the kings, princes, and generals hide after the earthquake?

2176. What is the number of those who were sealed from all the tribes of Israel?

2177. How many thousands were sealed in each of the twelve tribes found in Revelation 7?

2178. The great multitude before the throne wore white robes and carried what in their hands?

2179. Out of what significant trial did the great multitude come according to one of the elders in Revelation 7?

2180. By what did the robes of the great multitude get washed white in color?

2181. How long was there silence in heaven when the seventh seal was opened up?

2182. When the seventh seal was opened, what musical instruments were the seven angels given?

2183. What did the angel hurl at the earth?

2184. At the sounding of the first trumpet, what struck the earth?

2185. At the sounding of the second trumpet, something like a huge mountain was thrown into what?

2186. At the sounding of the third trumpet, what fell from the sky?

2187. What was the name of the great star that fell to earth in Revelation 8?

2188. When the great falling star struck the water, how did the water now taste in Revelation 8?

2189. At the sounding of the fourth trumpet, a third of what three things were turned dark?

2190. What bird, in Revelation 8, flew overhead and spoke to the inhabitants of the earth?

2191. At the fifth trumpet, what fell to earth and was given the key to the Abyss?

2192. When the fifth trumpet sounded in Revelation 9, what insects flew out of the smoke?

2193. How long did the locusts torture those without a seal on their head?

2194. The agony these locusts caused was like a sting from what creature?

2195. What was the Hebrew name of the king of the locusts?

2196. What was the Greek name of the king of the locusts?

2197. The sixth trumpet in Revelation released four angels from what river?

2198. These four angels killed what fraction of mankind?

2199. What three things came out of the mouths of the horses?

2200. The horses' tails resembled what other creature?

2201. What "little" object did the mighty angel in Revelation 10 hold in his hand?

2202. What two places did the mighty angel of Revelation 10 plant his feet?

2203. How many thunders spoke in Revelation 10?

2204. What flavor did the scroll taste like when John ate it in Revelation 10?

2205. But how would the scroll make his stomach feel?

2206. In Revelation 11, John was given a reed like a what?

2207. What was John told to measure?

2208. According to Revelation 11, how many months will the Gentiles trample the holy city?

2209. For how many days, according to Revelation 11, will the two witnesses prophesy?

2210. If anyone harms these witnesses, what will come from the witnesses' mouths?

2211. What will rise up from the Abyss and attack the witnesses?

2212. What was the figurative name for the great city where the witnesses are killed?

2213. How many days will the people celebrate their death?

2214. How did the people celebrate the death of the two witnesses in Revelation 11?

2215. What caused a tenth of the city to collapse?

2216. How many were killed in that devastation?

2217. In Revelation 12, what three celestial objects were wrapped around the woman, from her head to her feet?

2218. In Revelation 12, how many heads, horns, and crowns did the red dragon have?

2219. What fraction of stars did the dragon's tail wipe out of the sky?

2220. What did the woman give birth to?

2221. For how many days was the woman taken care of in the desert place?

2222. Who was the angel that fought against the dragon and his angels in Revelation 12?

2223. What two names did this ancient serpent also go by?

2224. In Revelation 12, the woman was given two wings like what great animal?

2225. What three animals are likened to the first beast in Revelation 13?

2226. What did one of the heads of the beast seem to have on it?

2227. What happened to the fatal wound on one of the heads of the beast?

2228. To whom did the dragon give authority, according to Revelation 13?

2229. How many months was the beast given a mouth to blasphemy?

2230. The second beast in Revelation 13 had horns like what animal?

2231. The second beast spoke like what creature?

2232. What happened to people who did not worship the image of the first beast?

2233. On what two parts of the body were the marks of the beast placed?

2234. Without this mark, someone could not do what two things?

2235. What was the number of the beast?

2236. On what mountain were the Lamb and the 144,000 standing in Revelation 14?

2237. What did the 144,000 not defile themselves with, which kept them pure?

2238. The second angel proclaimed that what "great" nation had fallen?

2239. What "maddening" beverage did Babylon the Great make the nations drink?

2240. What did the angel in Revelation 14 swing over the earth to reap the ripe harvest?

2241. To what height on a horse did the blood flow in Revelation 14?

2242. In Revelation 15, seven angels came out of the temple with seven what?

2243. What did the four living creatures give the seven angels that were filled with the wrath of God?

2244. During the first bowl of wrath, what appeared on people who had taken the mark of the beast?

2245. During the second bowl of wrath, what did the sea turn into?

2246. During the third bowl of wrath, what did the rivers and springs turn into?

2247. During the fourth bowl of wrath, what scorched the earth with fire?

2248. During the fifth bowl of wrath, what did the beast's kingdom plunge into?

2249. During the sixth bowl of wrath, what river dried up?

2250. In Revelation 16, what did the three evil spirits look like that came out of mouths?

2251. From the mouths of what three things did the evil spirits come?

2252. What was the Hebrew name of the place mentioned in Revelation 16 where the kings gathered together?

2253. During the seventh bowl of wrath, what occurrence struck so severely, nothing like it had ever happened on earth before?

2254. How many sections did the great city split into?

2255. About how much did the hailstones weigh that fell on men in Revelation 16?

2256. In Revelation 17, who committed adultery with the "great prostitute"?

2257. What was the color of the beast that the prostitute sat on?

2258. What was the beast covered with?

2259. How many heads and horns did the beast in Revelation 17 have?

2260. What three colors was the woman/prostitute dressed in?

2261. What was in the prostitute's hand?

2262. In Revelation 17, whose blood was the woman drunk with?

2263. The seven heads and the ten horns in Revelation 17 both represented what?

2264. What do the waters represent?

2265. Who did the woman represent at the end of Revelation 17?

2266. What is the name given to the great city in Revelation 18?

2267. What three professions wept greatly over the destruction of the great city in Revelation 18?

2268. In Revelation 18, what did the mighty angel pick up and throw into the sea?

2269. In Revelation 19, the bride was wearing fine linen, which stood for what?

2270. What was the name given to the rider of the white horse in Revelation 19:11?

2271. What was the robe of the rider dipped in from Revelation 19?

2272. What came out of the mouth of the white horse rider and was used to strike down the nations?

2273. In Revelation 19, the beast is captured along with who else?

2274. Where are they both thrown into?

2275. Once the enemies were killed in Revelation 19, what gorged on their flesh?

2276. In Revelation 20, the angel appeared out of heaven with what two things in his hands?

2277. What three names were attributed to the great dragon in Revelation 20?

2278. How many years did the angel bind the dragon into the Abyss?

2279. According to Revelation 20, how were the people killed because of their testimony for Jesus?

2280. What had they not worshipped?

2281. What two names did Revelation 20 give to the four corners of the earth where satan deceived?

2282. In Revelation 20, who is already in the lake of fire when the devil is thrown in?

2283. As the dead stand before the throne in Revelation 20, what are the deeds of dead recorded in?

2284. The lake of fire is also called the second what?

2285. Unless your name is written in the Book of Life, you are thrown into what?

2286. When the new heaven and new earth arrive, what part of creation does Revelation 21 say will no longer be?

2287. When the new heaven and new earth arrive, what will God wipe away from every eye?

2288. In heaven, what four things did Revelation 21:4 say would be no more?

2289. God used what two Greek words to describe himself as the beginning and the end?

2290. According to Revelation 21, where does the second death occur?

2291. How many gates did John see in Revelation 21 around the Holy City?

2292. Whose names were written on the gates around the Holy City in Revelation 21?

2293. How many gates pointed in all four directions?

2294. What was written on the twelve foundations of the Holy City in Revelation 21?

2295. What did the angel measure the city with?

2296. What shape was the city laid out in?

2297. How many different types of precious stones were found in the Holy City?

2298. What were the twelve gates made of in Revelation 21?

2299. What was the great street of the heavenly city made of in Revelation 21?

2300. What building structure did John not see in heaven?

2301. What two celestial bodies did the heavenly city not need?

2302. To live in heaven, your name needs to be written where?

2303. What flowed from the throne of God and down the middle of the great street of the city?

2304. What kind of tree was on each side of the river in Revelation 22?

2305. How many crops of fruit did the tree of life bear?

2306. What did the leaves of the tree of life provide healing for?

2307. Since God provided light, what did Revelation 22 say there would be no more of?

2308. How many times in Revelation 22 did Jesus say he was coming soon?

2309. In Revelation 22:13, Jesus called himself the _____ and the Omega, the first and the _____, the _____ and the end.

2310. What do the blessed do with their robes?

2311. What kind of animal did Jesus compare those who are outside the gates of the city to?

2312. In Revelation 22, Jesus called himself the Offspring of whom?

2313. What kind of star did Jesus describe himself as?

2314. What did the Spirit and the bride say to everyone who hears these words in Revelation 22?

2315. What free gift did Jesus offer at the end of Revelation 22?

2316. What is the last word of the last book in the Bible?

PART TWO

THE
ANSWERS

★THE★
Extreme
NEW TESTAMENT
Challenge

Matthew

1. Abraham (Matthew 1:2)
2. Judah (Matthew 1:2)
3. Tamar, Rahab, Ruth, Bathsheba, Mary (Matthew 1:3,5,6,16)
4. Tamar (Matthew 1:3)
5. Obed (Matthew 1:5)
6. Bathsheba, the wife of Uriah (Matthew 1:6)
7. Jacob (Matthew 1:16)
8. Fourteen (Matthew 1:17)
9. The Holy Spirit (Matthew 1:18)
10. Divorce her (Matthew 1:19)
11. An angel (Matthew 1:21)
12. Their sins (Matthew 1:21)
13. Isaiah (Matthew 1:23)
14. Immanuel (Matthew 1:23)
15. Bethlehem (Matthew 2:1)
16. Judea (Matthew 2:1)
17. Herod (Matthew 2:1)
18. East (Matthew 2:1)
19. A star (Matthew 2:2)
20. All of Jerusalem (Matthew 2:3)
21. Chief priests and teachers of the law (Matthew 2:4)
22. Micah (Matthew 2:5-6)
23. A house (Matthew 2:11)
24. Gold, incense/frankincense, myrrh (Matthew 2:11)
25. A dream (Matthew 2:12)
26. A dream (Matthew 2:13)
27. Hosea (Matthew 2:15)
28. Herod died (Matthew 2:15)
29. Two years old (Matthew 2:16)
30. Jeremiah (Matthew 2:17)
31. Four (Matthew 1:20, 2:13,19,22)
32. Archelaus (Matthew 2:22)
33. Herod (Matthew 2:22)
34. Nazareth (Matthew 2:23)
35. Galilee (Matthew 2:22-23)
36. A Nazarene (Matthew 2:23)
37. Isaiah (Matthew 3:3)
38. Camel hair (Matthew 3:4)
39. Leather (Matthew 3:4)
40. Locusts and honey (Matthew 3:4)
41. The Jordan (Matthew 3:6)
42. Pharisees and Sadducees (Matthew 3:7)
43. Good fruit (Matthew 3:10)
44. The Holy Spirit and fire (Matthew 3:11)
45. At the baptism of Jesus and the transfiguration of Jesus (Matthew 3:17, 17:5)
46. The Spirit of God (Matthew 3:16)
47. Forty days and nights (Matthew 4:2)
48. Bread (Matthew 4:3)
49. Every word that comes from the mouth of God (Matthew 4:4)
50. The Temple (Matthew 4:5)
51. Jump/throw himself down (Matthew 4:6)

52. Angels (Matthew 4:6)

53. Psalm 91 (Matthew 4:6)

54. Deuteronomy (Matthew 4:4,7,10)

55. Angels (Matthew 4:11)

56. Capernaum (Matthew 4:13) 57. Isaiah (Matthew 4:14)

58. Sea of Galilee (Matthew 4:18)

59. Andrew (Matthew 4:18)

60. Fishermen (Matthew 4:18)

61. James and John (Matthew 4:21)

62. Fishermen (Matthew 4:21)

63. Their nets (Matthew 4:21)

64. Their boat and their father (Matthew 4:22)

65. Syria (Matthew 4:24)

66. The kingdom of heaven (Matthew 5:3)

67. Those who mourn (Matthew 5:3)

68. The earth (Matthew 5:5)

69. Righteousness (Matthew 5:6)

70. The pure in heart (Matthew 5:8)

71. Peacemakers (Matthew 5:9)

72. Salt (Matthew 5:13)

73. A light (Matthew 5:15)

74. Their good deeds (Matthew 5:16)

75. The law and the prophets (Matthew 5:17)

76. The Pharisees, and the teachers, of the law (Matthew 5:20)

77. Raca (Matthew 5:22)

78. Eye and hand (Matthew 5:29-30)

79. Right hand (Matthew 5:30)

80. Sexual immorality (Matthew 5:32)

81. Heaven, earth, Jerusalem, your head (Matthew 5:34-36)

82. Left (Matthew 5:39)

83. Coat/cloak (Matthew 5:40)

84. Tax collectors (Matthew 5:46)

85. Our acts of righteousness (Matthew 6:1)

86. Trumpets (Matthew 6:2)

87. Streets and synagogues (Matthew 6:5)

88. Pagans (Matthew 6:7)

89. Bread (Matthew 6:11)

90. Put oil on your head and wash your face (Matthew 6:17)

91. Moth (Matthew 6:19)

92. The eye (Matthew 6:22)

93. God and money (Matthew 6:24)

94. Birds, lilies, grass (Matthew 6:26,28)

95. His kingdom and his righteousness (Matthew 6:33)

96. Plank/stick of wood (Matthew 7:3)

97. Pearls (Matthew 7:6)

98. Stone (Matthew 7:9)

99. Snake (Matthew 7:10)

100. Destruction (Matthew 7:13)

101. Life (Matthew 7:14)

102. Sheep's clothing (Matthew 7:15)

103. Wolves (Matthew 7:15)

104. By their fruit (Matthew 7:16)

105. Prophesying, casting out demons, performing miracles (Matthew 7:22)

106. Rock (Matthew 7:24)

107. Rain, flood, wind (Matthew 7:25)

108. Authority (Matthew 7:29)

109. Leprosy (Matthew 8:3)

110. His servant (Matthew 8:6)

111. A Roman centurion (Matthew 8:10)

112. Peter (Matthew 8:14)

113. Fever (Matthew 8:14)

114. Her hand (Matthew 8:15)

115. She got up and waited on Jesus (Matthew 8:15)

116. Foxes and birds (Matthew 8:20)

117. Sleeping (Matthew 8:24)

118. Two (Matthew 8:28)

119. The cemetery/tombs (Matthew 8:28)

120. Pigs (Matthew 8:30)

121. Leave (Matthew 8:34)

122. Forgive him of his sins (Matthew (9:2-3)

123. His mat (Matthew 9:6)

124. A tax collector's booth (Matthew 9:9)

125. Tax collectors and sinners (Matthew 9:10)

126. Matthew's house (Matthew 9:10)

127. A doctor (Matthew 9:12)

128. Sacrifice (Matthew 9:13)

129. Sinners (Matthew 9:13)

130. Unshrunk cloth (Matthew 9:16)

131. Old wineskins (Matthew 9:17)

132. A synagogue leader (Matthew 9:18)

133. Twelve years (Matthew 9:20)

134. Jesus' cloak (Matthew 9:21)

135. Pipes (Matthew 9:23)

136. Asleep (Matthew 9:24)

137. They laughed (Matthew 9:24)

138. Son of David (Matthew 9:27)

139. Demon possession (Matthew 9:32)

140. Workers (Matthew 9:37)

141. Peter/Simon (Matthew 10:2)

142. Simon the Zealot (Matthew 10:4)

143. Judas Iscariot (Matthew 10:4)

144. Samaritans (Matthew 10:5)

145. The lost sheep of Israel (Matthew 10:6)

146. Gold, silver, copper, bag, extra tunic/ shirt, sandals, staff (Matthew 10:9-10)

147. Shake the dust off their feet (Matthew 10:14)

148. Sodom and Gomorrah (Matthew 10:15)

149. A snake (Matthew 10:16)

150. A dove (Matthew 10:16)

151. Synagogues (Matthew 10:17)

152. The Holy Spirit (Matthew 10:20)

153. The soul (Matthew 10:28)

154. Two (Matthew 10:29)

155. The hairs on our head (Matthew 10:30)

156. A sword (Matthew 10:34)

157. Father, mother, son, and daughter (Matthew 10:37)

158. Their cross (Matthew 10:38)

159. A cup of cold water (Matthew 10:42)

160. A reed (Matthew 11:7)

161. A prophet (Matthew 11:9)

162. Malachi (Matthew 11:10)

163. John the Baptist (Matthew 11:14)

164. A glutton and a drunk (Matthew 11:19)

165. Korazin and Bethsaida (Matthew 11:21-22)

166. Capernaum (Matthew 11:23-24)

167. Little children (Matthew 11:25)

168. Yoke (Matthew 11:29)

169. Our souls (Matthew 11:29)

170. Grain (Matthew 12:1)

171. David (Matthew 12:3-4)

172. Sheep (Matthew 12:11)

173. His hand (Matthew 12:13)

174. Reed (Matthew 12:20)

175. Wick (Matthew 12:20)

176. satan/Beelzebub (Matthew 12:24)

177. The Holy Spirit (Matthew 12:31)

178. Every careless word (Matthew 12:36)

179. Wicked and adulterous (Matthew 12:39)

180. Jonah (Matthew 12:40)

181. Seven (Matthew 12:44-45)

182. Birds (Matthew 13:4)

183. The Good News/the message (Matthew 13:19)

184. The cares of the world/riches (Matthew 13:22)

185. Thirty, sixty, a hundred (Matthew 13:23)

186. Weeds (Matthew 13:25)

187. Mustard seed (Matthew 13:32)

188. Yeast (Matthew 13:33)

189. The world (Matthew 13:38)

190. The people of the kingdom (Matthew 13:38)

191. satan (Matthew 13:3)

192. Angels (Matthew 13:39)

193. A hidden treasure (Matthew 13:44)

194. James, Joseph, Simon, Judas (Matthew 13:57)

195. A prophet (Matthew 13:57)

196. Miracles (Matthew 13:58)

197. Herod Antipas/the Tetrarch (Matthew 14:1)

198. Herodias (Matthew 14:3)

199. They were brothers (Matthew 14:3)

200. Herodias' (Matthew 14:6)

201. Herod's birthday (Matthew 14:6)

202. John the Baptist (Matthew 14:9-10)

203. Prison (Matthew 14:10)

204. A platter (Matthew 14:11)

205. His disciples (Matthew 14:1

206. Five fish and two loaves of b
(Matthew 14:17)

207. Twelve baskets (Matthew 14

208. Dawn/fourth watch
(Matthew 14:25)

209. A ghost (Matthew 14:26)

210. Peter (Matthew 14:28)

211. The wind (Matthew 14:30)

212. The edge of his cloak
(Matthew 14:36)

213. The Pharisees (Matthew 15:

214. Pits (Matthew 15:14)

215. Demon possession
(Matthew 15:22)

216. The dogs (Matthew 15:26)

217. The crumbs (Matthew 15:27)

218. Three days (Matthew 15:32)

219. Seven (Matthew 15:34)

220. Seven (Matthew 15:37)

221. Red (Matthew 16:2)

222. Pharisees and Sadducees
(Matthew 16:12)

223. John the Baptist, Elijah, Jeremiah
(Matthew 16:14)

224. Rock (Matthew 16:18)

225. Hades (Matthew 16:18)

226. satan (Matthew 16:23)

227. Peter, James, John (Matthew 17:1)

228. The sun (Matthew 17:2)

229. Moses and Elijah (Matthew 17:3)

253. A hundred times more
(Matthew 19:29)

254. A denarius or a full day's wa
(Matthew 20:9)

255. Zebedee's (Matthew

256. A slave (Matthe

257. His life (M

258. A don

259. Z

26

241. Heaven (Matthew 18:18)

242. Two (Matthew 18:19)

243. Seven times (Matthew 18:21)

244. Seventy-seven times
(Matthew 18:21)

245. Ten thousand bags of gold/talents
(Matthew 18:24)

246. A hundred silver coins/denarii
(Matthew 18:28)

247. Because of people's hard hearts
(Matthew 19:8)

248. Marital unfaithfulness
(Matthew 19:9)

249. The poor (Matthew 19:21)

250. The rich (Matthew 19:23)

251. The eye of a needle
(Matthew 19:24)

252. The twelve tribes of Israel
(Matthew 19:28)

ges

20:20)

w 20:27)

atthew 20:28)

ey and a colt (Matthew 21:2)

echariah (Matthew 21:5)

0. Cloaks and tree branches/palms (Matthew 21:8)

261. Save/save us (Matthew 21:9)

262. Doves (Matthew 21:12)

263. Robbers/thieves (Matthew 21:13)

264. Fig (Matthew 21:19)

265. John the Baptist's (Matthew 21:25)

266. Tax collectors and prostitutes (Matthew 21:31)

267. His son (Matthew 21:37)

268. Killed him (Matthew 21:39)

269. The capstone/cornerstone (Matthew 21:42)

270. A king (Matthew 22:2)

271. A wedding for his son (Matthew 22:2)

272. They ignored, mistreated and killed them (Matthew 22:5-6)

273. The streets/street corners (Matthew 22:9-10)

274. Wedding clothes (Matthew 22:11)

275. Into the outer darkness, the place of weeping and gnashing of teeth (Matthew 22:13)

276. Denarius (Matthew 22:19)

277. Caesar's (Matthew 22:21)

278. Sadducees (Matthew 22:23)

279. Seven brothers (Matthew 22:25)

280. The angels (Matthew 22:30)

281. An expert in the law (Matthew 22:35)

282. David's son (Matthew 22:42)

283. A finger (Matthew 23:4)

284. Phylacteries or prayer boxes (Matthew 23:5)

285. Rabbi (Matthew 23:7)

286. Seven (Matthew 23:13-29)

287. Hell (Matthew 23:15)

288. Mint, dill, cumin (Matthew 23:23)

289. Camel (Matthew 23:24)

290. Cup and the dish (Matthew 23:25)

291. Tombs (Matthew 23:27)

292. Snakes/vipers (Matthew 23:33)

293. Abel and Zechariah (Matthew 23:35)

294. A hen and her chicks (Matthew 23:37)

295. The temple (Matthew 24:2)

296. Mount of Olives (Matthew 24:3)

297. Wars (Matthew 24:6)

298. Love (Matthew 24:12)

299. Pregnant and nursing mothers (Matthew 24:19)

300. Messiahs and prophets (Matthew 24:24)

301. Sun and the moon (Matthew 24:29)

302. Jesus' words (Matthew 24:35)

303. The father (Matthew 24:36)

304. Noah (Matthew 24:37)

305. A field (Matthew 24:40)

306. A hand mill (Matthew 24:41)

307. Ten (Matthew 25:1)

308. Five and five (Matthew 25:2)

309. Oil (Matthew 25:3)

310. Midnight (Matthew 25:6)

311. According to their ability (Matthew 25:15)

312. Dug a hole and hid it (Matthew 25:18)

313. Good, faithful (Matthew 25:23)

314. A hard man (Matthew 25:24)

315. Outside into darkness (Matthew 25:30)

316. Sheep and goats (Matthew 25:32)

317. Hungry, thirsty, a stranger, naked, in prison (Matthew 25:35-36)

318. Passover (Matthew 26:2)

319. Caiaphas, the High Priest's (Matthew 26:3)

320. Simon the leper's (Matthew 26:6)

321. On the poor (Matthew 26:8-9)

322. Thirty pieces of silver (Matthew 26:15)

323. Bowl (Matthew 26:23)

324. Judas and Peter (Matthew 26:25,34)

325. The Mount of Olives (Matthew 26:30)

326. Gethsemane (Matthew 26:36)

327. The cup (Matthew 26:39,42)

328. Three times (Matthew 26:40,43,44)

329. Swords and clubs (Matthew 26:47)

330. A kiss (Matthew 26:48)

331. His ear (Matthew 26:51)

332. Twelve legions (Matthew 26:53)

333. Caiaphas (Matthew 26:57)

334. The temple (Matthew 26:61)

335. A servant girl (Matthew 26:69)

336. Another servant girl (Matthew 26:71)

337. His accent (Matthew 26:73)

338. Curses (Matthew 26:74)

339. Three times (Matthew 26:75)

340. A rooster (Matthew 26:75)

341. He threw them into the temple (Matthew 27:5)

342. By hanging (Matthew 27:5)

343. Field of Blood/Potter's Field/ Akeldama (Matthew 27:8-10)

344. Jeremiah (Matthew 27:9)

345. Pilate (Matthew 27:11)

346. Barabbas (Matthew 27:17)

347. His wife (Matthew 27:19)

348. "Crucify him!" (Matthew 27:23)

349. Wash his hands (Matthew 27:24)

350. Scarlet (Matthew 27:28)

351. Cyrene (Matthew 27:32)

352. Golgotha (Matthew 27:33)

353. Place of the skull (Matthew 27:33)

354. Wine/vinegar mixed with gall (Matthew 27:34)

355. Robbery/rebellion (Matthew 27:38)

356. Psalm 22 (Matthew 27:46)

357. Elijah (Matthew 27:47)

358. The temple curtain (Matthew 27:51)

359. A centurion and other guards (Matthew 27:54)

360. Mary Magdalene, Mary the mother of James and Joseph, and the mother of Zebedee's sons (Matthew 27:56)

361. Arimathea (Matthew 27:57-60)

362. Linen (Matthew 27:59)

363. Sealed the tomb and posted guards (Matthew 27:65)

364. Lightning (Matthew 28:3)

365. Snow (Matthew 28:3)

366. Galilee (Matthew 28:7,10)

367. His followers stole him at night (Matthew 28:13)

368. Galilee (Matthew 28:16)

369. Go, make disciples, baptize, teach (Matthew 28:19-20)

Mark

370. Isaiah (Mark 1:2-3)

371. Baptism of repentance for the forgiveness of sins (Mark 1:4)

372. Jordan (Mark 1:5)

373. Camel (Mark 1:6)

374. A leather belt (Mark 1:6)

375. Locusts and honey (Mark 1:6)

376. The thong/strap (Mark 1:7)

377. The Holy Spirit (Mark 1:8)

378. The Spirit (Mark 1:10)

379. Wild animals and angels (Mark 1:13)

380. Fishermen (Mark 1:16,19)

381. Their nets (Mark 1:18)

382. Zebedee (Mark 1:20)

383. A demon (Mark 1:25-26)

384. Peter's (Mark 1:30)

385. A fever (Mark 1:30)

386. She waited on them (Mark 1:31)

387. Who he was (Mark 1:34)

388. Leprosy (Mark 1:41-42)

389. The priest (Mark 1:44)

390. Capernaum (Mark 2:1-3)

391. Forgave his sins (Mark 2:5)

392. Alphaeus (Mark 2:14, 3:18)

393. Tax collectors and sinners (Mark 2:15)

394. The sick (Mark 2:17)

395. Fast (Mark 2:18)

396. Old wineskins (Mark 2:22)

397. Working on the Sabbath (Mark 2:24)

398. Shriveled hand (Mark 3:3)

399. The Herodians (Mark 3:6)

400. Sons of Thunder (Mark 3:17)

401. Beelzebub, the Prince of Demons (Mark 3:22)

402. A kingdom, a house, satan (Mark 3:24-26)

403. The Holy Spirit (Mark 3:29)

404. God's will (Mark 3:34)

405. Rocky, hardened path, thorny, good soil (Mark 4:4-8)

406. Bird (Mark 4:4)

407. Thirty, sixty, one hundred times more (Mark 4:8)

408. Hear (Mark 4:9)

409. The people who have received the word (Mark 4:15)

410. satan (Mark 4:15)

411. Trouble or persecution (Mark 4:17)

412. Worries of this life, deceitfulness of wealth, and desires for other things (Mark 4:19)

413. On a stand (Mark 4:21)

414. A mustard seed (Mark 4:31)

415. A cushion (Mark 4:38)

416. The wind and the waves (Mark 4:41)

417. Gerasenes/Gadarenes/Gergesenes (Mark 5:1)

418. The tombs (Mark 5:3)

419. Chains/irons (Mark 5:3-4)

420. Legion (Mark 5:9)

421. Because there were many of them (Mark 5:9)

422. 2,000 pigs (Mark 5:13)

423. They wanted him to leave town (Mark 5:17)

424. The Decapolis (Mark 5:20)

425. Jairus (Mark 5:22-23)

426. Synagogue leader (Mark 5:22)

427. Twelve years (Mark 5:25)

428. Jesus' cloak/tunic (Mark 5:27)

429. Peter, James, John (Mark 5:37)

430. Talitha Kuom/Get up, little girl (Mark 5:41)

431. Twelve years old (Mark 5:42)

432. Carpenter (Mark 6:3)

433. James, Joseph, Judas, Simon (Mark 6:3)

434. His sisters (Mark 6:3)

435. His hometown (Mark 6:1,4)

436. Their lack of faith (Mark 6:6)

437. The dust (Mark 6:11)

438. John the Baptist had risen from the dead, Elijah or one of the prophets of long ago (Mark 6:14-15)

439. Herodias (Mark 6:17)

440. Herod's brother's wife (Mark 6:17)

441. Philip (Mark 6:17)

442. His birthday (Mark 6:21-22)

443. Up to half his kingdom (Mark 6:23)

444. The head of John the Baptist (Mark 6:25)

445. A platter (Mark 6:25)

446. His disciples (Mark 6:29)

447. A shepherd (Mark 6:34)

448. Half a year's wage/eight months (Mark 6:37)

449. Five loaves (Mark 6:38)

450. Two fish (Mark 6:38)

451. Hundreds and fifties (Mark 6:40)

452. Twelve baskets (Mark 6:43)

453. Men (Mark 6:44)

454. Late at night/the fourth watch (Mark 6:48)

455. A ghost (Mark 6:49)

456. Isaiah (Mark 7:6)

457. Corban (Mark 7:11)

458. Greek/Syrophoenician (Mark 7:26-28)

459. Her daughter (Mark 7:29)

460. The man's ears and tongue (Mark 7:33)

461. Ephphatha (Mark 7:34)

462. Be opened (Mark 7:34)

463. Three days (Mark 8:2)

464. Seven loaves (Mark 8:5)

465. A few small fish (Mark 8:7)

466. Seven basketfuls (Mark 8:8)

467. Pharisees and Herod (Mark 8:15)

468. Jesus spit on the man's eyes and put his hands on him (Mark 8:23)

469. Trees walking around (Mark 8:24)

470. Caesarea Philippi (Mark 8:27)

471. John the Baptist, Elijah, one of the prophets (Mark 8:28)

472. Peter (Mark 8:32)

473. satan (Mark 8:33)

474. Human concerns (Mark 8:33)

475. Their souls (Mark 8:36)

476. Peter, James, John (Mark 9:2)

477. White (Mark 9:3)

478. Moses and Elijah (Mark 9:4)

479. Peter (Mark 9:5)

480. Elijah (Mark 9:11-12)

481. Fire and water (Mark 9:22)

482. His unbelief (Mark 9:24)

483. Prayer (Mark 9:29)

484. A child (Mark 9:36-37)

485. A cup of water (Mark 9:41)

486. A millstone (Mark 9:42)

487. Hand, foot, eye (Mark 9:43-47)

488. Moses (Mark 10:5)

489. The disciples (Mark 10:13)

490. He blessed them (Mark 10:16)

491. The commandments (Mark 10:19-20)

492. In heaven (Mark 10:21)

493. A rich man (Mark 10:25)

494. Fields and homes (Mark 10:29-30)

495. One hundred times (Mark 10:29-30)

496. Mock him, spit on him, flog him, kill him (Mark 10:34)

497. James and John (Mark 10:35)

498. One at his right and one at his left (Mark 10:37)

499. Bartimaeus (Mark 10:46)

500. Son of Timaeus (Mark 10:46)

501. His faith (Mark 10:52)

502. It had never been ridden (Mark 11:2)

503. Cloaks and branches (Mark 11:8)

504. Bethany (Mark 11:11)

505. It was not the season (Mark 11:13)

506. He stopped them from carrying merchandise (Mark 11:16)

507. A den of thieves/robbers (Mark 11:17)

508. A mountain (Mark 11:23)

509. Was John's baptism from heaven or from men? (Mark 11:30)

510. Three servants plus many others (Mark 12:2-5)

511. His son (Mark 12:6)

512. The cornerstone/capstone (Mark 12:10)

513. A denarius (Mark 12:15)

514. Caesar's (Mark 12:16)

515. They believed there was no resurrection (Mark 12:18)

516. Seven brothers (Mark 12:20)

517. Angels (Mark 12:25)

518. Deuteronomy 6:4-5 and Leviticus 19:18 (Mark 12:31-32)

519. Two coins (Mark 12:42)

520. Copper (Mark 12:42)

521. The Mount of Olives (Mark 13:3-4)

522. They would be flogged (Mark 13:9)

523. The Holy Spirit (Mark 13:11)

524. Pregnant women and nursing mothers (Mark 13:17)

525. Winter (Mark 13:18)

526. Clouds (Mark 13:26)

527. A fig tree (Mark 13:28)

528. His words (Mark 13:31)

529. Simon the leper's (Mark 14:3)

530. Alabaster (Mark 14:3)

531. Pure nard (Mark 14:3)

532. The poor (Mark 14:5)

533. A jar of water (Mark 14:13)

534. Bread (Mark 14:20)

535. His body (Mark 14:22)

536. His blood (Mark 14:23-25)

537. Sang a hymn (Mark 14:26)

538. Gethsemane (Mark 14:36)

539. A rooster (Mark 14:30)

540. Three times (Mark 14:37-41)

541. Swords and clubs (Mark 14:43)

542. A kiss (Mark 14:44)

543. Servant of the high priest (Mark 14:47)

544. A linen garment (Mark 14:51)

545. People needed to give false statements (Mark 14:56-57)

546. A servant girl (Mark 14:66-69)

547. Galilee (Mark 14:70)

548. Twice (Mark 14:72)

549. Barabbas (Mark 15:7)

550. Insurrection and murder (Mark 15:7)

551. Envy (Mark 15:10)

552. The chief priests (Mark 15:11)

553. Praetorium (Mark 15:16)

554. Purple (Mark 15:17)

555. Cyrene (Mark 15:21)

556. Simon (Mark 15:21)

557. Alexander and Rufus (Mark 15:21)

558. Place of the Skull (Mark 15:22)

559. Myrrh (Mark 15:23)

560. Third hour/nine in the morning (Mark 15:25)

561. King of the Jews (Mark 15:26)

562. Robbers/thieves/rebels (Mark 15:27)

563. Insults (Mark 15:29)

564. Sixth hour/noon (Mark 15:33)

565. Ninth/three o'clock in the afternoon (Mark 15:33)

566. Elijah (Mark 15:35)

567. A Roman centurion (Mark 15:39)

568. Mary Magdalene, Mary mother of James and Joseph, Salome (Mark 15:40)

569. Joseph of Arimathea (Mark 15:43)

570. The Council (Mark 15:43)

571. Pilate (Mark 15:45)

572. Linen (Mark 15:46)

573. Mary Magdalene and Mary mother of Joseph (Mark 15:47)

574. Spices (Mark 16:1)

575. A rock (Mark 16:3)

576. A young man in white/an angel (Mark 16:5)

577. Galilee (Mark 16:7)

578. Seven demons (Mark 16:9)

Luke

579. Careful investigation (Luke 1:3)

580. Theopolis (Luke 1:3)

581. Zechariah (Luke 1:5)

582. Priest (Luke 1:5)

583. Elizabeth (Luke 1:5)

584. Aaron's/Levi's (Luke 1:5)

585. To burn incense (Luke 1:9)

586. John (Luke 1:13)

587. Wine or fermented drink (Luke 1:15)

588. Elijah (Luke 1:17)

589. Malachi (Luke 1:17)

590. Gabriel (Luke 1:19)

591. He would be unable to speak (Luke 1:20)

592. Nazareth (Luke 1:26)

593. Joseph (Luke 1:27)

594. The throne of David (Luke 1:27)

595. Jacob's (Luke 1:33)

596. She was a virgin (Luke 1:34)

597. The Holy Spirit (Luke 1:35)

598. Elizabeth's (Luke 1:41)

599. Three months (Luke 1:56)

600. Zechariah (Luke 1:59)

601. John (Luke 1:63)

602. Mary and Zechariah (Luke 1:46,67)

603. He was able to talk (Luke 1:64)

604. The desert/wilderness (Luke 1:80)

605. Augustus (Luke 2:1)

606. Quirinius (Luke 2:2)

607. Bethlehem (Luke 2:4)

608. David (Luke 2:4)

609. Cloths (Luke 2:7)

610. A manger (Luke 2:7)

611. Shepherds (Luke 2:8-10)

612. One angel (Luke 2:9)

613. A child wrapped in cloths and lying in a manger (Luke 2:12)

614. In her heart (Luke 2:19)

615. A great company/host of angels (Luke 2:13)

616. Eight days (Luke 2:21)

617. Eight days (Luke 2:21)

618. Consecration/dedication of the firstborn male (Luke 2:22-23)

619. Two young pigeons or doves (Luke 2:24)

620. Simeon and Anna (Luke 2:25,36)

621. See the Lord's child/Messiah (Luke 2:26)

622. The Holy Spirit (Luke 2:26)

623. Anna (Luke 2:36)

624. Seven years (Luke 2:36)

625. Nazareth (Luke 2:39)

626. Passover (Luke 2:41-42)

627. Twelve years old (Luke 2:42)

628. One day's travel (Luke 2:44)

629. Three days (Luke 2:46)

630. In the temple courts (Luke 2:46)

631. The teachers of the law (Luke 2:46)

632. They were amazed at his understanding and answers (Luke 2:47)

633. In his father's house (Luke 2:49)

634. Tiberius (Luke 3:1)

635. Pilate (Luke 3:1)

636. Herod (Luke 3:1)

637. Annas and Caiaphas (Luke 3:2)

638. Isaiah (Luke 3:4)

639. Stones (Luke 3:8)

640. Tax collectors and soldiers (Luke 3:12)

641. Soldiers (Luke 3:14)

642. His sandals/shoes (Luke 3:16)

643. The Holy Spirit and fire (Luke 3:16)

644. Herodias, his brother's wife (Luke 3:19)

645. A dove (Luke 3:22)

646. Thirty years old (Luke 3:23)

647. Joseph (Luke 3:23)

648. God (Luke 3:37)

649. Forty days (Luke 4:2)

650. Deuteronomy (Luke 4:4,8,12)

651. Bread (Luke 4:3)

652. All the kingdoms of the world (Luke 4:5)

653. Jerusalem temple (Luke 4:9)

654. Isaiah (Luke 4:17)

655. A cliff (Luke 4:29)

656. A high fever (Luke 4:38)

657. "You are the Son of God" (Luke 4:41)

658. Sea of Galilee (Luke 5:1)

659. Washing them (Luke 5:2)

660. They began to sink (Luke 5:7)

661. Simon Peter (Luke 5:8)

662. James and John (Luke 5:10)

663. People (Luke 5:10)

664. Leprosy (Luke 5:13-14)

665. The tiles (Luke 5:19)

666. He forgave the man's sins (Luke 5:20)

667. A tax booth (Luke 5:27)

668. Tax collectors and sinners (Luke 5:20)

669. A doctor (Luke 5:31)

670. Old wineskins (Luke 5:37)

671. Pick heads of grain (Luke 6:1-2)

672. A man with a shriveled hand (Luke 6:6,10)

673. Simon, James, Judas (Luke 6:14)

674. Your shirt/tunic (Luke 6:29)

675. Sinners (Luke 6:32)

676. Your lap (Luke 6:38)

677. A pit (Luke 6:39)

678. A plank (Luke 6:41)

679. Bad fruit (Luke 6:43)

680. His heart (Luke 6:45)

681. Rock (Luke 6:48)

682. Centurion (Luke 7:3)

683. Say the word (Luke 7:7)

684. Nain (Luke 7:11-12)

685. His coffin/bier (Luke 7:14)

686. John the Baptist's (Luke 7:20)

687. A reed swayed by the wind and a man dressed in fine clothes (Luke 7:24-25)

688. Malachi (Luke 7:27)

689. John the Baptist (Luke 7:28)

690. Glutton, drunkard, friend of sinners (Luke 7:34)

691. A Pharisee's house (Luke 7:36-37)

692. Alabaster (Luke 7:37)

693. Perfume (Luke 7:37)

694. His feet (Luke 7:38,45)

695. Mary Magdalene, Joanna, Susanna (Luke 8:2-3)

696. Seven (Luke 8:2)

697. Herod's (Luke 8:3)

698. Birds (Luke 8:5)

699. They had no moisture (Luke 8:6)

700. Thorns (Luke 8:7)

701. A hundred times (Luke 8:8)

702. The word of God (Luke 8:11)

703. The devil (Luke 8:12)

704. Life's worries, riches, pleasures (Luke 8:14)

705. Under a clay jar or under a bed (Luke 8:16)

706. Those who hear the word of God and put it into practice (Luke 8:21)

707. The winds and the water (Luke 8:25)

708. Gerasenes (Luke 8:26-27)

709. In tombs (Luke 8:27)

710. Chains on his hands and feet (Luke 8:29)

711. Legion (Luke 8:30)

712. The abyss (Luke 8:31)

713. Into the pigs (Luke 8:32)

714. They asked him to leave (Luke 8:37)

715. Go home and tell people what God did for him (Luke 8:38-39)

716. Jairus (Luke 8:41)

717. Twelve years old (Luke 8:42)

718. Peter, John, James (Luke 8:51)

719. Twelve years (Luke 8:43)

720. His cloak (Luke 8:44)

721. Power (Luke 8:46)

722. Asleep (Luke 8:52)

723. No staff, bag, bread, money, extra tunic (Luke 9:3)

724. The dust (Luke 9:5)

725. John the Baptist (Luke 9:7)

726. Bethsaida (Luke 9:10)

727. Five loaves and two fish (Luke 9:13)

728. The men (Luke 9:14)

729. About fifty (Luke 9:14)

730. Twelve baskets (Luke 9:17)

731. Elijah, John the Baptist, one of the prophets (Luke 9:19)

732. They will lose it (Luke 9:24)

733. He will be ashamed of them (Luke 9:26)

734. Peter, James, John (Luke 9:28)

735. Flashes of lightning (Luke 9:29)

736. Moses and Elijah (Luke 9:30)

737. The Mount of Transfiguration and the garden of Gethsamane (Luke 9:32, 22:45)

738. Shelters (Luke 9:33)

739. Screams, convulses, foams at the mouth (Luke 9:39)

740. Who was greatest (Luke 9:46)

741. Fire (Luke 9:54)

742. A place to lay his head (Luke 9:58)

743. Seventy-two people (Luke 10:1)

744. Workers (Luke 10:2)

745. Wolves (Luke 10:3)

746. Purse, bag, and sandals (Luke 10:4)

747. Dust (Luke 10:11)

748. Chorazin, Bethsaida, Capernaum (Luke 10:13,15)

749. Sodom, Tyre, Sidon (Luke 10:12,13)

750. Demons (Luke 10:17)

751. satan (Luke 10:18)

752. Snakes and scorpions (Luke 10:19)

753. Prophets and kings (Luke 10:24)

754. Jericho (Luke 10:30)

755. A priest and a Levite (Luke 10:31-32)

756. Oil and wine (Luke 10:34)

757. Two denarii/two silver coins (Luke 10:35)

758. Mary sat while Martha worked (Luke 10:39-40)

759. Bread (Luke 11:5)

760. An egg (Luke 11:12)

761. Beezelbub (Luke 11:15)

762. Seven other demons (Luke 11:26)

763. The sign of Jonah (Luke 11:29)

764. The Queen of the South/Sheba (Luke 11:31)

765. Nineveh (Luke 11:32)

766. The eye (Luke 11:34)

767. He didn't wash his hands (Luke 11:38)

768. A cup and a dish (Luke 11:39)

769. The best seats and respectful greetings (Luke 11:43)

770. Abel and Zechariah (Luke 11:50)

771. The Pharisees' (Luke 12:1)

772. Hell (Luke 12:5)

773. Five sparrows (Luke 12:6)

774. Hair (Luke 12:7)

775. The Holy Spirit (Luke 12:10)

776. Possessions (Luke 12:15)

777. Barns (Luke 12:18)

778. Flowers/lilies (Luke 12:27)

779. Grass (Luke 12:28)

780. Their heart (Luke 12:34)

781. Much more (Luke 12:48)

782. Division (Luke 12:51)

783. Daughter-in-law (Luke 12:53)

784. The weather (Luke 12:56)

785. Eighteen people (Luke 13:4)

786. Eighteen years (Luke 13:11)

787. Untying a donkey and leading it to water (Luke 13:15)

788. A mustard seed (Luke 13:18-19)

789. A fox (Luke 13:32)

790. Jerusalem (Luke 13:34)

791. Dropsy/Abnormal swelling of his body (Luke 14:2)

792. A child and an ox (Luke 14:5)

793. At the lowest place (Luke 14:10)

794. The poor, crippled, lame, and blind (Luke 14:13)

795. A field (Luke 14:18)

796. Five yoke of oxen (Luke 14:19)

797. The streets and alleys of the town (Luke 14:21)

798. The roads and country lanes (Luke 14:23)

799. Their own cross (Luke 14:27)

800. A tower (Luke 14:28)

801. The soil or the manure pile (Luke 14:35)

802. Luke (Luke 15)

803. The Pharisees and teachers of the law (Luke 15:2)

804. Ninety-nine sheep (Luke 15:4)

805. On his shoulders (Luke 15:5)

806. Heaven (Luke 15:7)

807. Ten coins (Luke 15:8)

808. Silver (Luke 15:8)

809. Younger (Luke 15:12)

810. Wild living/prostitutes (Luke 15:13,30)

811. A famine (Luke 15:14)

812. Pigs (Luke 15:16)

813. Robe, ring, sandals (Luke 15:22)

814. Music and dancing (Luke 15:25)

815. A goat (Luke 15:29)

816. Found (Luke 15:32)

817. Olive oil (Luke 16:6)

818. 800 bushels (Luke 16:7)

819. God and money (Luke 16:13)

820. Heaven and earth (Luke 16:17)

821. Purple (Luke 16:19)

822. Dogs (Luke 16:21)

823. Abraham (Luke 16:22)

824. Dip his finger in water and cool the man's tongue (Luke 16:24)

825. Lazarus or someone from the dead (Luke 16:27,30)

826. Five brothers (Luke 16:28)

827. Moses and the prophets (Luke 16:31)

828. A millstone (Luke 17:2)

829. Each time, so seven (Luke 17:4)

830. Mustard (Luke 17:6)

831. Mulberry tree (Luke 17:6)

832. Ten (Luke 17:12)

833. Samaria (Luke 17:16)

834. Noah and Lot (Luke 17:26,28)

835. In bed and grinding grain (Luke 17:34-35)

836. Vultures (Luke 17:37)

837. A judge (Luke 18:2)

838. Robbers, evildoers, adulterers (Luke 18:11)

839. A little child (Luke 18:16-17)

840. Sell everything and give to the poor (Luke 18:22)

841. The rich (Luke 18:25)

842. Blindness (Luke 18:35,41)

843. Jericho (Luke 19:1)

844. Chief tax collector (Luke 19:2)

845. He was short (Luke 19:3)

846. A sycamore/fig tree (Luke 19:4)

847. Four times (Luke 19:8)

848. Salvation (Luke 19:9)

849. Ten servants (Luke 19:13)

850. Ten minas (Luke 19:13)

851. Ten cities (Luke 19:17)

852. They were given to a servant with ten minas (Luke 19:24)

853. The Mount of Olives (Luke 19:29)

854. No one had ever ridden it (Luke 19:30)

855. Their cloaks (Luke 19:35)

856. The stones/rocks (Luke 19:40)

857. The city (Luke 19:41)

858. Robbers/thieves (Luke 19:46)

859. Heaven or man (Luke 20:4)

860. The vineyard owner's son (Luke 20:14-15)

861. The stone the builders rejected (Luke 20:17-18)

862. Denarius (Luke 20:24)

863. Caesar's portrait (Luke 20:25)

864. Sadducees (Luke 20:27)

865. Seven brothers (Luke 20:29)

866. Angels (Luke 20:36)

867. Widow's houses (Luke 20:47)

868. Make lengthy prayers (Luke 20:47)

869. Two small copper coins (Luke 21:2)

870. Jerusalem (Luke 21:20)

871. Pregnant women and nursing mothers (Luke 21:23)

872. In the sun, moon, and stars (Luke 21:25)

873. Jesus' words (Luke 21:33)

874. Judas Iscariot (Luke 22:3)

875. The Day of Unleavened Bread (Luke 22:7)

876. Peter and John (Luke 22:8)

877. A jar of water (Luke 22:10)

878. The kingdom of God (Luke 22:18)

879. Who was greatest (Luke 22:24)

880. Simon Peter (Luke 22:31)

881. Prison and death (Luke 22:33)

882. Three (Luke 22:34)

883. A sword (Luke 22:36)

884. Two swords (Luke 22:38)

885. Temptation (Luke 22:40)

886. This cup (Luke 22:43)

887. Blood (Luke 22:44)

888. The right ear (Luke 22:50)

889. He healed the man (Luke 22:51)

890. A servant girl (Luke 22:56)

891. Jesus (Luke 22:61)

892. The Messiah and the Son of God (Luke 22:67,70)

893. He opposed paying taxes to Caesar and he claimed to be the Messiah (Luke 23:2)

894. Herod (Luke 23:7)

895. A sign (Luke 23:8)

896. Herod and Pilate (Luke 23:12)

897. Barabbas (Luke 23:18)

898. Insurrection and murder (Luke 23:19)

899. Simon from Cyrene (Luke 23:26)

900. By casting lots (Luke 23:34)

901. Wine vinegar (Luke 23:36)

902. "This is the King of the Jews" (Luke 23:38)

903. In paradise (Luke 23:43)

904. Three hours, from noon to three (Luke 23:44)

905. The curtain (Luke 23:45)

906. The Centurion (Luke 23:47)

907. Arimathea (Luke 23:51)

908. Spices and perfumes (Luke 23:56)

909. Two (Luke 24:4)

910. Lightning (Luke 24:4)

911. Mary Magdalene, Joanna, Mary the mother of James (Luke 24:10)

912. Emmaus (Luke 24:13)

913. Seven miles (Luke 24:13)

914. Cleopas (Luke 24:18)

915. Bread (Luke 24:30)

916. He broke bread, gave thanks and gave it to them (Luke 24:30,35)

917. A ghost (Luke 24:37)

918. Flesh and bones (Luke 24:39)

919. Broiled fish (Luke 24:42-43)

920. Their minds (Luke 24:45)

John

924. Genesis 1:1 (John 1:1)

925. Darkness (John 1:5)

926. John (John 1:6)

927. Children of God (John 1:12)

928. Flesh (John 1:14)

929. Grace and truth (John 1:17)

930. The Messiah, Elijah, the Prophet (John 1:20,21)

931. Isaiah (John 1:23)

932. His sandals (John 1:27)

933. Bethany beyond the Jordan (John 1:28)

934. The sin of the world (John 1:29)

935. The Spirit (John 1:32-33)

936. Andrew (John 1:35,40)

937. Peter, his brother (John 1:41-42)

938. Cephas/Peter (John 1:42)

939. Bethsaida (John 1:44)

940. Nathanael (John 1:46)

941. Philip (John 1:46)

942. Under a fig tree (John 1:48)

943. Angels of God (John 1:51)

944. Cana (John 2:1)

945. Galilee (John 2:1)

946. The third day (John 2:1-2)

921. Power from on high (Luke 24:49)

922. Bethany (Luke 24:50)

923. Praise God (Luke 24:53)

947. Six stone jars (John 2:6)

948. Twenty to thirty gallons (John 2:6)

949. The master of the banquet (John 2:9)

950. Cattle, sheep, doves (John 2:14)

951. A whip (John 2:15)

952. Three days (John 2:19)

953. Forty-six years (John 2:20)

954. His body (John 2:21)

955. Nicodemus (John 3:1-2)

956. Pharisee and member of the Jewish ruling council (John 3:1-2)

957. Jesus performed signs (John 3:2)

958. Born again (John 3:3)

959. A mother's womb (John 3:4)

960. Wind (John 3:8)

961. The snake (John 3:14)

962. Condemn it (John 3:17)

963. Their deeds (John 3:20)

964. Aenon near Salim (John 3:23)

965. John the Baptist (John 3:30)

966. His disciples (John 4:2)

967. Sychar (John 4:5)

968. They would get thirsty again (John 4:13)

969. They would never thirst again (John 4:14)

970. Five (John 4:18)

971. Spirit, truth (John 4:23)

972. Christ (John 4:25)

973. Her water jug (John 4:28)

974. To do the will of God (John 4:34)

975. Ripe for harvest (John 4:35)

976. Capernaum (John 4:46-47)

977. Cana (John 4:46)

978. Cana (John 4:46)

979. The healing of the royal official's son (John 4:54)

980. Bethesda (John 5:2)

981. Five (John 5:2)

982. Thirty-eight years (John 5:5)

983. For the waters to be stirred so he could get in (John 5:7)

984. He picked up his mat (John 5:10)

985. Father (John 5:18)

986. The graves (John 5:28-29)

987. John the Baptist (John 5:32-33)

988. The Scriptures (John 5:39)

989. Moses (John 5:46)

990. The Sea of Galilee (John 6:1)

991. Philip (John 6:5)

992. More than a year/eight months (John 6:7)

993. Andrew (John 6:8)

994. Five small loaves and two small fish (John 6:9)

995. Barley (John 6:9)

996. Twelve baskets (John 6:13)

997. King (John 6:15)

998. Three to four miles (John 6:19)

999. The feeding of the 5,000 (John 6:26)

1000. Moses (John 6:32-33)

1001. Bread (John 6:35)

1002. His flesh and his blood (John 6:54)

1003. Judas (John 6:71)

1004. Simon Iscariot (John 6:71)

1005. The Feast of the Tabernacles (John 7:2-3)

1006. Circumcision (John 7:22-23)

1007. Rivers/streams of living water (John 7:38)

1008. The Holy Spirit (John 7:38)

1009. Galilee (John 7:41-42)

1010. The temple guards (John 7:45)

1011. The woman caught in adultery (John 8:1-11)

1012. Draw in the dirt (John 8:6)

1013. Stones (John 8:7)

1014. The Father and himself (John 8:14)

1015. The truth (John 8:32)

1016. Abraham (John 8:39)

1017. The devil (John 8:44)

1018. Death (John 8:51)

1019. Abraham (John 8:58-59)

1020. So God might be displayed in his life (John 9:3)

1021. Mud and spit (John 9:6)

1022. Siloam (John 9:7)

1023. Sent (John 9:7)

1024. Because he healed on the Sabbath (John 9:16)

1025. His parents (John 9:18)

1026. The synagogue (John 9:22)

1027. Blind, see (John 9:25)

1028. His voice (John 10:4)

1029. The Gate for the Sheep and the Good Shepherd (John 10:7,11)

1030. A wolf (John 10:12)

1031. His life (John 10:17-18)

1032. The Father (John 10:30)

1033. Stone him (John 10:33)

1034. Bethany (John 11:1)

1035. She poured perfume on Jesus and wiped his feet with her hair (John 11:2)

1036. Two days (John 11:6)

1037. He said Lazarus was asleep (John 11:11-13)

1038. Didymus (John 11:16)

1039. Four days (John 11:17)

1040. Two miles (John 11:18)

1041. Both Mary and Martha (John 11:21,32)

1042. Martha (John 11:24)

1043. Lazarus (John 11:25)

1044. Lazarus (John 11:35)

1045. "Lazarus, come out!" (John 11:43)

1046. Strips of linen and a cloth on his face (John 11:44)

1047. Caiaphas (John 11:50)

1048. Mary (John 12:3)

1049. Pure nard (John 12:3)

1050. Judas Iscariot (John 12:4)

1051. The poor (John 12:5)

1052. Judas Iscariot (John 12:6)

1053. Because he used to help himself to the money (John 12:6)

1054. Lazarus (John 12:10)

1055. Zechariah (John 12:15, Zechariah 9:9)

1056. Philip (John 12:20)

1057. Wheat (John 12:24)

1058. Isaiah (John 12:40-41)

1059. Human praise (John 12:42)

1060. Judas (John 13:2)

1061. A towel (John 13:4)

1062. Peter (John 13:8)

1063. His hands and head (John 13:9)

1064. Bread (John 13:26)

1065. Judas Iscariot (John 13:26)

1066. Simon (John 13:26)

1067. satan (John 13:27)

1068. Judas (John 13:29)

1069. Love one another (John 13:34)

1070. Rooster (John 13:38)

1071. A place for them with him (John 14:2)

1072. Way, truth, life (John 14:6)

1073. Philip (John 14:8)

1074. The miracles/the works (John 14:11)

1075. The Holy Spirit (John 14:26)

1076. Peace (John 14:27)

1077. The gardener (John 15:1)

1078. He cuts them off (John 15:2)

1079. He prunes them (John 15:2)

1080. The branches (John 15:4)

1081. Fruit (John 15:8)

1082. Laying down his life (John 15:13)

1083. Servants (John 15:14-15)

1084. The Counselor/Advocate/the Holy Spirit (John 15:26)

1085. The Counselor/the Holy Spirit (John 16:7)

1086. Sin, righteousness, judgment (John 16:8)

1087. The pain of labor (John 16:21)

1088. The world (John 16:35)

1089. Destruction (John 17:12)

1090. The Kidron Valley (John 18:1)

1091. They often went there (John 18:2)

1092. Torches, lanterns, weapons (John 18:3)

1093. They fell to the ground (John 18:6)

1094. Peter (John 18:10)

1095. The right ear (John 18:10)

1096. The high priest (John 18:10)

1097. Malchus (John 18:10)

1098. Annas, the high priest (John 18:13)

1099. Caiaphas (John 18:13)

1100. A servant girl (John 18:16-17)

1101. The high priest's courtyard (John 18:15)

1102. A fire (John 18:18)

1103. Caiaphas (John 18:24)

1104. The man whose ear Peter cut off (John 18:26)

1105. Passover (John 18:28)

1106. Pilate (John 18:38)

1107. Barabbas (John 18:40)

1108. A rebellion (John 18:40)

1109. Thorns (John 19:2)

1110. Purple (John 19:2)

1111. Pilate (John 19:5)

1112. Caesar (John 19:12)

1113. Stone Pavement (John 19:13)

1114. Gabbatha (John 19:13)

1115. Caesar (John 19:15)

1116. The Skull (John 19:17)

1117. Golgotha (John 19:17)

1118. Aramaic, Latin, Greek (John 19:20)

1119. Four parts (John 19:23)

1120. His undergarment (John 19:23)

1121. The undergarment (John 19:23-24)

1122. Mary (John 19:25)

1123. Mary his mother, Mary the wife of Clopas, Mary Magdalene (John 19:25)

1124. The disciple whom Jesus loved (John 19:26)

1125. Wine vinegar (John 19:29)

1126. A sponge (John 19:29)

1127. The stalk of a hyssop plant (John 19:29)

1128. His legs (John 19:33)

1129. One of the soldiers (John 19:34)

1130. Blood and water (John 19:34)

1131. Joseph of Arimathea (John 19:38)

1132. Seventy-five pounds (John 19:39)

1133. Mary Magdalene (John 20:1-2)

1134. Peter (John 20:6)

1135. Strips of linen and the burial cloth (John 20:7)

1136. Two angels (John 20:12)

1137. White (John 20:12)

1138. The gardener (John 20:15)

1139. Mary Magdalene (John 20:15)

1140. Rabboni (John 20:16)

1141. The Jewish leaders (John 20:19)

1142. "Peace be with you" (John 20:19,21,26)

1143. His hands and his side (John 20:25)

1144. A week (John 20:26)

1145. "My Lord and my God" (John 20:28)

1146. Didymus (John 21:2)

1147. Cana (John 21:2)

1148. Bread and fish (John 21:9)

1149. 153 (John 21:11)

1150. Three times (John 21:14)

1151. Three times (John 21:15-17)

1152. Peter and the disciple Jesus loved/ John (John 21:19,23)

1153. Books (John 21:25)

Acts

1154. Theophilus (Acts 1:1)

1155. Forty days (Acts 1:3)

1156. Jerusalem (Acts 1:4)

1157. The Holy Spirit (Acts 1:5)

1158. Jerusalem, Judea, Samaria, the ends of the earth (Acts 1:8)

1159. Two men (Acts 1:10)

1160. The sky (Acts 1:11)

1161. Mount of Olives (Acts 1:12)

1162. Mary mother of Jesus and his brothers (Acts 1:14)

1163. One hundred and twenty men (Acts 1:15)

1164. He fell headlong, his body burst open and his intestines spilled out (Acts 1:18)

1165. Akeldama or Field of Blood (Acts 1:19)

1166. Matthias and Barsabbas (Acts 1:23)

1167. Joseph or Justus (Acts 1:23)

1168. By casting lots (Acts 1:26)

1169. Matthias (Acts 1:26)

1170. Pentecost (Acts 2:1)

1171. A violent wind (Acts 2:2)

1172. A house (Acts 2:2)

1173. Tongues of fire (Acts 2:3)

1174. Galilee (Acts 2:7)

1175. Wine (Acts 2:13)

1176. Peter (Acts 2:14)

1177. Nine in the morning (Acts 2:15)

1178. Joel (Acts 2:16)

1179. His Spirit (Acts 2:18)

1180. Psalms, 16 and 110 (Acts 2:23-28, 34-35)

1181. Be baptized (Acts 2:38)

1182. Three thousand (Acts 2:41)

1183. Their own possessions (Acts 2:45)

1184. Beautiful (Acts 3:2)

1185. Money (Acts 3:3)

1186. Moses and Samuel (Acts 3:22,24)

1187. Five thousand men (Acts 4:4)

1188. Peter and John (Acts 4:6-7)

1189. They were unschooled, ordinary men (Acts 4:13)

1190. Over forty years old (Acts 4:22)

1191. It was shaken (Acts 4:31)

1192. Barnabas (Acts 4:36)

1193. Son of encouragement (Acts 4:36)

1194. A field (Acts 4:37)

1195. Ananias (Acts 5:1)

1196. A piece of property (Acts 5:2)

1197. satan (Acts 5:3)

1198. The Holy Spirit/God (Acts 5:3-4)

1199. He died on the spot (Acts 5:5)

1200. Three hours later (Acts 5:7)

1201. She would die (Acts 5:9-10)

1202. Solomon's Colonnade (Acts 5:12)

1203. Peter's (Acts 5:15)

1204. An angel (Acts 5:19)

1205. The temple courts (Acts 5:20)

1206. Gamaliel (Acts 5:34)

1207. Theudas and Judas the Galilean (Acts 5:34, 36)

1208. They were flogged (Acts 5:40)

1209. The Grecian/Hellenistic Jews (Acts 6:1)

1210. Seven (Acts 6:3)

1211. Stephen, Philip, Procorus, Nicanor, Timon, Parmenas, Nicolas (Acts 6:5)

1212. Stephen (Acts 6:5)

1213. The Synagogue of Freedmen (Acts 6:9)

1214. The Sanhedrin (Acts 6:12)

1215. An angel (Acts 6:15)

1216. Forty years—birth to murder of Egyptian, going to Midian to the burning bush, in the wilderness with the Israelites (Acts 7:23,30,36)

1217. Their teeth (Acts 7:54)

1218. Jesus (Acts 7:55)

1219. Their ears (Acts 7:57)

1220. Saul (Acts 7:58)

1221. Judea and Samaria (Acts 8:1)

1222. Saul (Acts 8:3)

1223. Samaria (Acts 8:5)

1224. Simon (Acts 8:9)

1225. Philip (Acts 8:12-13)

1226. Peter and John (Acts 8:14)

1227. Money (Acts 8:18)

1228. An Ethiopian eunuch (Acts 8:27)

1229. All the treasury of the queen of Ethiopia (Acts 8:27)

1230. Isaiah (Acts 8:28)

1231. A chariot (Acts 8:30)

1232. Water (Acts 8:36)

1233. Azotus (Acts 8:40)

1234. Caesarea (Acts 8:40)

1235. Damascus (Acts 9:2)

1236. The way (Acts 9:2)

1237. Jesus (Acts 9:5)

1238. His sight (Acts 9:9)

1239. Three days (Acts 9:9)

1240. Ananias (Acts 9:10)

1241. Judas' (Acts 9:11)

1242. Straight Street (Acts 9:11)

1243. Tarsus (Acts 9:11)

1244. Scales (Acts 9:18)

1245. He was baptized (Acts 9:18)

1246. In a basket (Acts 9:25)

1247. Barnabas (Acts 9:27)

1248. Grecian/Hellenistic Jews (Acts 9:29)

1249. Aeneas (Acts 9:33)

1250. Tabitha/Dorcas (Acts 9:36)

1251. Simon (Acts 9:43)

1252. Cornelius (Acts 10:1,3,5)

1253. The Italian regiment (Acts 10:1)

1254. Simon the tanner's (Acts 10:6)

1255. A sheet (Acts 10:11)

1256. Four-footed animals, reptiles, and birds (Acts 10:12)

1257. Three times (Acts 10:16)

1258. A Gentile (Acts 10:28)

1259. Stephen's (Acts 11:19)

1260. Tarsus (Acts 11:25)

1261. Antioch (Acts 11:26)

1262. Agabus (Acts 11:27)

1263. Claudius (Acts 11:28)

1264. King Herod (Acts 12:1-2)

1265. By sword (Acts 12:2)

1266. An angel (Acts 12:11)

1267. Mary, the mother of John/Mark (Acts 12:12)

1268. Rhoda (Acts 12:13)

1269. His angel (Acts 12:15)

1270. The guards (Acts 12:19)

1271. People of Tyre and Sidon (Acts 12:20)

1272. His royal robes (Acts 12:21)

1273. He did not give praise to God (Acts 12:23)

1274. An angel struck him and he was eaten by worms (Acts 12:23)

1275. It spread and flourished (Acts 12:24)

1276. John/Mark (Acts 12:25)

1277. Barnabas and Saul (Acts 13:2)

1278. John/Mark (Acts 13:5,13)

1279. Bar-Jesus/Elymas (Acts 13:6,8)

1280. Sergius Paulus (Acts 13:7)

1281. Sorcerer (Acts 13:8)

1282. Blindness (Acts 13:11)

1283. Perga in Pamphylia (Acts 13:13)

1284. Seven nations (Acts 13:19)

1285. The Jews (Acts 13:45)

1286. Gentiles (Acts 13:46-48)

1287. God-fearing women and high-standing men (Acts 13:50)

1288. The Jewish synagogue (Acts 14:1)

1289. Lystra and Derbe (Acts 14:6)

1290. Faith (Acts 14:9)

1291. Zeus (Acts 14:12)

1292. Hermes (Acts 14:12)

1293. He got up and went back into the city (Acts 14:20)

1294. Elders (Acts 14:23)

1295. They needed to be circumcised (Acts 15:1)

1296. They were given the Holy Spirit (Acts 15:8)

1297. Paul, Peter, and James (Acts 15:7,12,13)

1298. Food for idols, sexual immorality, the meat of strangled animals, and blood (Acts 15:20)

1299. Judas/Barsabbas and Silas (Acts 15:22)

1300. John/Mark (Acts 15:37-39)

1301. Silas (Acts 15:40)

1302. A Greek (Acts 16:1)

1303. Circumcise him (Acts 16:3)

1304. Galatia and Philippi (Acts 16:6,12)

1305. Bithynia (Acts 16:7)

1306. Macedonia (Acts 16:9)

1307. Lydia (Acts 16:14)

1308. Purple cloth (Acts 16:14)

1309. Fortune telling/telling the future (Acts 16:16)

1310. Praying and singing hymns (Acts 16:25)

1311. An earthquake (Acts 16:26)

1312. Fall on his sword/kill himself (Acts 16:27)

1313. The jailer (Acts 16:29-30)

1314. To his home (Acts 16:34)

1315. They were Roman citizens (Acts 16:37-38)

1316. Jason's (Acts 17:6)

1317. The Bereans (Acts 17:11)

1318. The Thessalonians (Acts 17:11)

1319. Epicurean and Stoic philosophers (Acts 17:18)

1320. Athens (Acts 17:19)

1321. To an unknown god (Acts 17:23)

1322. Dionysius and Damaris (Acts 17:34)

1323. Corinth (Acts 18:1-2)

1324. Claudius ordered all Jews to leave (Acts 18:2)

1325. A tentmaker (Acts 18:3)

1326. Crispus (Acts 18:8)

1327. One and a half years (Acts 18:11)

1328. Gallio (Acts 18:12)

1329. He had his hair cut off (Acts 18:18)

1330. Apollos (Acts 18:24-26)

1331. John's (Acts 18:25)

1332. The Holy Spirit (Acts 19:2)

1333. John's baptism (Acts 19:3)

1334. A baptism of repentance (Acts 19:4)

1335. They spoke in tongues and prophesied (Acts 19:6)

1336. Twelve (Acts 19:7)

1337. Three months (Acts 19:8)

1338. Tyrannus (Acts 19:9)

1339. Jews and Greeks (Acts 19:10)

1340. Handkerchiefs and aprons (Acts 19:12)

1341. Sceva (Acts 19:14)

1342. Naked and bleeding (Acts 19:16)

1343. Their scrolls (Acts 19:19)

1344. 50,000 drachmas (Acts 19:19)

1345. Timothy and Erastus (Acts 19:22)

1346. Demetrius (Acts 19:24)

1347. Silver shrines (Acts 19:24)

1348. Artemis (Acts 19:27,35)

1349. Gaius and Aristarchus (Acts 19:29)

1350. Alexander (Acts 19:33-34)

1351. Two hours (Acts 19:34)

1352. The City Clerk (Acts 19:35,41)

1353. It fell from heaven (Acts 19:35)

1354. In a legal assembly (Acts 19:39)

1355. Eutychus (Acts 20:9)

1356. Three stories (Acts 20:9)

1357. Ephesus (Acts 20:17,38)

1358. Jesus (Acts 20:35)

1359. Philip (Acts 21:8-9)

1360. Agabus (Acts 21:10-11)

1361. Jerusalem (Acts 21:11)

1362. The temple (Acts 21:27)

1363. Roman guards (Acts 21:35)

1364. Tarsus in Cilicia (Acts 22:3)

1365. Gamaliel (Acts 22:3)

1366. Roman (Acts 22:28)

1367. He told them he was a Roman citizen (Acts 22:29)

1368. The high priest Ananias (Acts 23:2)

1369. Paul (Acts 23:6)

1370. Sadducees (Acts 23:8)

1371. Rome (Acts 23:11)

1372. Eat or drink (Acts 23:12)

1373. The son of Paul's sister (Acts 23:16)

1374. Felix (Acts 23:24)

1375. Tertullus (Acts 24:1)

1376. Drusilla (Acts 24:24)

1377. A bribe (Acts 24:26)

1378. Porcius Festus (Acts 24:27)

1379. Jerusalem (Acts 25:1-2)

1380. Caesar (Acts 25:11)

1381. King Agrippa and Bernice (Acts 25:23)

1382. Aramaic (Acts 26:14)

1383. A Christian (Acts 26:28)

1384. Appealed to Caesar (Acts 26:32)

1385. Julius (Acts 27:1)

1386. Aristarchus (Acts 27:2)

1387. The pilot and the owner of the ship (Acts 27:11)

1388. Northeaster/hurricane (Acts 27:14)

1389. Ropes (Acts 27:17)

1390. Caesar (Acts 27:24)

1391. Adriatic Sea (Acts 27:27)

1392. Fourteen days (Acts 27:33)

1393. 276 (Acts 27:37)

1394. Malta (Acts 28:1)

1395. A viper (Acts 28:3)

1396. Publius (Acts 28:7)

1397. Fever/dysentery (Acts 28:8)

1398. Castor and Pollux (Acts 28:11)

1399. Two years (Acts 28:30)

Romans

1400. The Gospel (Romans 1:1)

1401. The Gentiles (Romans 1:5)

1402. Some spiritual gift (Romans 1:11)

1403. Salvation (Romans 1:16)

1404. His eternal power and divine nature (Romans 1:20)

1405. Images (Romans 1:23)

1406. Humans, birds, animals, and reptiles (Romans 1:23)

1407. A lie (Romans 1:25)

1408. A depraved mind (Romans 1:28)

1409. Ourselves (Romans 2:1)

1410. Wrath (Romans 2:5)

1411. According to what they have done (Romans 2:6)

1412. Obey the law (Romans 2:13)

1413. Their hearts (Romans 2:15)

1414. Themselves (Romans 2:21)

1415. Circumcision (Romans 2:25)

1416. A Jew (Romans 2:28-29)

1417. The Jews (Romans 3:2)

1418. Truthfulness/glory (Romans 3:7)

1419. Psalms, Ecclesiastes, Isaiah (Romans 3:10-18)

1420. Grave (Romans 3:13)

1421. Their feet (Romans 3:15)

1422. The glory of God (Romans 3:23)

1423. His blood (Romans 3:25)

1424. Faith (Romans 3:28)

1425. An obligation (Romans 4:4)

1426. Righteousness (Romans 4:3)

1427. Circumcision (Romans 4:10-11)

1428. Wrath (Romans 4:15)

1429. Transgression (Romans 4:15)

1430. One hundred years old (Romans 4:19)

1431. Peace (Romans 5:1)

1432. Suffering (Romans 5:3)

1433. Character and hope (Romans 5:4)

1434. A good/righteous person (Romans 5:7)

1435. Died for us (Romans 5:8)

1436. One man (Romans 5:15)

1437. One sin (Romans 5:16)

1438. One man (Romans 5:19)

1439. Grace (Romans 5:20)

1440. Sinning (Romans 6:1)

1441. His resurrection (Romans 6:5)

1442. Death (Romans 6:9)

1443. Righteousness (Romans 6:18)

1444. Eternal life (Romans 6:23)

1445. An adulteress (Romans 7:3)

1446. Sin (Romans 7:7)

1447. Sin (Romans 7:8)

1448. Sin (Romans 7:16-17)

1449. Life and peace (Romans 8:6)

1450. Slaves (Romans 8:15)

1451. Abba Father (Romans 8:15)

1452. That we are God's children (Romans 8:16)

1453. Heirs (Romans 8:17)

1454. Sufferings (Romans 8:17)

1455. Future glory (Romans 8:18)

1456. Creation (Romans 8:20)

1457. Childbirth (Romans 8:22)

1458. The Spirit (Romans 8:26)

1459. Groans (Romans 8:26)

1460. Purpose (Romans 8:28)

1461. Interceding for us (Romans 8:34)

1462. Conquerors (Romans 8:37)

1463. Height and depth (Romans 8:39)

1464. The people of Israel (Romans 9:3)

1465. The promise (Romans 9:8)

1466. Common (Romans 9:21)

1467. The stone/rock (Romans 9:32-33)

1468. Israelites (Romans 10:1)

1469. Knowledge (Romans 10:2)

1470. "Jesus is Lord" (Romans 10:9)

1471. God raised Jesus from the dead (Romans 10:9)

1472. Our heart (Romans 10:10)

1473. Our mouth (Romans 10:10)

1474. They will be saved (Romans 10:13)

1475. Good news (Romans 10:15)

1476. His hands (Romans 10:21)

1477. Benjamin (Romans 11:1)

1478. Elijah (Romans 11:2-4)

1479. Works (Romans 11:6)

1480. Israel (Romans 11:11)

1481. An olive tree (Romans 11:17)

1482. The root (Romans 11:17-18)

1483. Gentiles (Romans 11:25)

1484. Living sacrifices (Romans 12:1)

1485. The pattern of this world (Romans 12:2)

1486. By the renewing of our mind (Romans 12:2)

1487. God's will (Romans 12:2)

1488. Body (Romans 12:5)

1489. Rejoicing (Romans 12:15)

1490. God's wrath (Romans 12:19)

1491. Feed them and give them something to drink (Romans 12:20)

1492. Burning coals (Romans 12:20)

1493. Good (Romans 12:21)

1494. Governing authorities (Romans 13:1)

1495. Our conscience (Romans 13:5)

1496. Taxes, revenue, respect, honor (Romans 13:7)

1497. Light (Romans 13:12)

1498. The Lord Jesus Christ (Romans 13:14)

1499. Vegetables (Romans 14:2)

1500. Eating and drinking (Romans 14:17)

1501. Eat meat, drink wine (Romans 14:21)

1502. The Gentiles (Romans 15:8)

1503. Where Christ was not known (Romans 15:20)

1504. Spain (Romans 15:24)

1505. Macedonia and Achaia (Romans 15:26)

1506. A deacon (Romans 16:1)

1507. Priscilla and Aquila (Romans 16:3)

1508. Epenetus (Romans 16:5)

1509. Smooth talk and flattery (Romans 16:18)

1510. satan (Romans 16:20)

1511. Timothy (Romans 16:21)

1512. Tertius (Romans 16:22)

1513. Erastus (Romans 16:24)

1 Corinthians

1514. Sosthenes (1 Corinthians 1:1)

1515. Any spiritual gift (1 Corinthians 1:7)

1516. Chloe's (1 Corinthians 1:11)

1517. Paul, Apollos, Cephas, Christ (1 Corinthians 1:12)

1518. Crispus and Gaius (1 Corinthians 1:14)

1519. Stephanas' (1 Corinthians 1:16)

1520. Preach the gospel (1 Corinthians 1:17)

1521. Signs (1 Corinthians 1:22)

1522. Wisdom (1 Corinthians 1:22)

1523. The wise and the strong (1 Corinthians 1:27)

1524. Eloquence or human wisdom (1 Corinthians 2:1)

1525. Wise and persuasive words (1 Corinthians 2:4)

1526. The mind of Christ (1 Corinthians 2:16)

1527. Milk (1 Corinthians 3:2)

1528. Apollos (1 Corinthians 3:6)

1529. God (1 Corinthians 3:6)

1530. Jesus Christ (1 Corinthians 3:11)

1531. Gold, silver, costly stones, wood, hay, straw (1 Corinthians 3:12)

1532. Fire (1 Corinthians 3:13)

1533. God's temple (1 Corinthians 3:16)

1534. The apostles
(1 Corinthians 4:12-13)

1535. Timothy (1 Corinthians 4:17)

1536. Talk (1 Corinthians 4:20)

1537. A whip/rod of discipline
(1 Corinthians 4:21)

1538. His father's (1 Corinthians 5:1)

1539. satan (1 Corinthians 5:5)

1540. Sexual immorality
(1 Corinthians 5:11)

1541. The world and angels
(1 Corinthians 6:2-3)

1542. Court (1 Corinthians 6:6)

1543. A prostitute (1 Corinthians 6:15)

1544. Sexual sins (1 Corinthians 6:18)

1545. The Holy Spirit (1 Corinthians 6:19)

1546. Have sexual relations with a woman
(1 Corinthians 7:1)

1547. A husband with his wife and a wife
with her husband
(1 Corinthians 7:2)

1548. Her/his body (1 Corinthians 7:4)

1549. During a time of prayer
(1 Corinthians 7:5)

1550. Self-control (1 Corinthians 7:5)

1551. Passion (1 Corinthians 7:9)

1552. Keeping God's commands
(1 Corinthians 7:19)

1553. Until he dies (1 Corinthians 7:39)

1554. Puffs up (1 Corinthians 8:1)

1555. Idols/gods (1 Corinthians 8:10)

1556. Meat (1 Corinthians 8:13)

1557. The Lord's brothers and Cephas/
Peter (1 Corinthians 9:5)

1558. To save some (1 Corinthians 9:22)

1559. The prize (1 Corinthians 9:24)

1560. A crown (1 Corinthians 9:25)

1561. A boxer (1 Corinthians 9:26)

1562. Christ (1 Corinthians 10:4)

1563. What we can bear
(1 Corinthians 10:13)

1564. A way out (1 Corinthians 10:13)

1565. The cup of demons
(1 Corinthians 10:21)

1566. Beneficial and constructive
(1 Corinthians 10:23)

1567. Do not eat it (1 Corinthians 10:28)

1568. Jews, Greek, the church of God
(1 Corinthians 10:32)

1569. His head (1 Corinthians 11:4)

1570. Long hair (1 Corinthians 11:15)

1571. His death (1 Corinthians 11:26)

1572. Eat the bread and take the cup/
takes communion
(1 Corinthians 11:28)

1573. Wisdom (1 Corinthians 12:8)

1574. Interpretation of tongues
(1 Corinthians 12:10)

1575. A hand (1 Corinthians 12:15)

1576. An eye (1 Corinthians 12:16)

1577. The hand (1 Corinthians 12:21)

1578. The feet (1 Corinthians 12:21)

1579. Apostles (1 Corinthians 12:28)

1580. Those who speak in tongues
(1 Corinthians 12:28)

1581. A resounding gong or clanging
cymbal (1 Corinthians 13:1)

1582. Patience (1 Corinthians 13:4)

1583. Wrongs (1 Corinthians 13:5)

1584. Prophecies, tongues, knowledge
(1 Corinthians 13:8)

1585. Face-to-face (1 Corinthians 13:12)

1586. Faith, hope, and love
(1 Corinthians 13:13)

1587. Love (1 Corinthians 13:13)

1588. Prophecy (1 Corinthians 14:1)

1589. The church (1 Corinthians 14:4)

1590. Five (1 Corinthians 14:19)

1591. Unbelievers (1 Corinthians 14:22)

1592. Interpreters (1 Corinthians 14:28)

1593. Peace (1 Corinthians 14:33)

1594. A woman speaking in church
(1 Corinthians 14:35)

1595. Her husband (1 Corinthians 14:35)

1596. Cephas/Peter (1 Corinthians 15:5)

1597. Five hundred (1 Corinthians 15:6)

1598. They have fallen asleep/died
(1 Corinthians 15:6)

1599. An apostle (1 Corinthians 15:9)

1600. Because he persecuted the church
(1 Corinthians 15:9)

1601. Our preaching and our faith
(1 Corinthians 15:14)

1602. Adam (1 Corinthians 15:22)

1603. Death (1 Corinthians 15:26)

1604. Wild beasts (1 Corinthians 15:32)

1605. Bad company
(1 Corinthians 15:33)

1606. Animals, birds, fish
(1 Corinthians 15:39)

1607. Heavenly bodies
(1 Corinthians 15:40)

1608. Imperishable (1 Corinthians 15:42)

1609. Heaven (1 Corinthians 15:47)

1610. Flesh and blood
(1 Corinthians 15:50)

1611. A trumpet (1 Corinthians 15:52)

1612. Victory (1 Corinthians 15:54)

1613. Sin (1 Corinthians 15:56)

1614. The law (1 Corinthians 15:56)

1615. Galatian (1 Corinthians 16:1)

1616. Macedonia (1 Corinthians 16:5)

1617. Timothy and Apollos
(1 Corinthians 16:10,12)

1618. Stephanas' (1 Corinthians 16:15)

1619. Aquila and Priscilla
(1 Corinthians 16:19)

1620. Kiss (1 Corinthians 16:20)

2 Corinthians

1621. Asia (2 Corinthians 1:8)

1622. Macedonia (2 Corinthians 1:16)

1623. His Spirit (2 Corinthians 1:22)

1624. satan (2 Corinthians 2:11)

1625. Titus (2 Corinthians 2:13)

1626. Tablets of human hearts
(2 Corinthians 3:3)

1627. Of the letter/the law
(2 Corinthians 3:6)

1628. Moses (2 Corinthians 3:13-14)

1629. Jars of clay (2 Corinthians 4:7)

1630. What is unseen, not seen
(2 Corinthians 4:18)

1631. Tent (2 Corinthians 5:1)

1632. Human hands (2 Corinthians 5:1)

1633. The Spirit (2 Corinthians 5:5)

1634. The Lord (2 Corinthians 5:6)

1635. Sight (2 Corinthians 5:7)

1636. At home with the Lord
(2 Corinthians 5:8)

1637. Creation (2 Corinthians 5:17)

1638. Reconciliation
(2 Corinthians 5:18-19)

1639. The righteousness of God
(2 Corinthians 5:21)

1640. A stumbling block
(2 Corinthians 6:3)

1641. Unbelievers (2 Corinthians 6:14)

1642. Titus (2 Corinthians 7:6,13,14)

1643. The previous letter he sent
(2 Corinthians 7:8-9)

1644. Repentance (2 Corinthians 7:8-9)

1645. Macedonia (2 Corinthians 8:1-2)

1646. Poor (2 Corinthians 8:9)

1647. Reaping and sowing
(2 Corinthians 9:6)

1648. A cheerful one (2 Corinthians 9:7)

1649. Every thought (2 Corinthians 10:5)

1650. His letters (2 Corinthians 10:9)

1651. The Lord (2 Corinthians 10:17)

1652. Jesus, the Spirit, and gospel
(2 Corinthians 11:4)

1653. Macedonia (2 Corinthians 11:9)

1654. An angel of light
(2 Corinthians 11:14)

1655. Lashings (2 Corinthians 11:24)

1656. Forty minus one
(2 Corinthians 11:24)

1657. Three times (2 Corinthians 11:25)

1658. Three times (2 Corinthians 11:25)

1659. His weakness
(2 Corinthians 11:30)

1660. In a basket (2 Corinthians 11:33)

1661. The third heaven
(2 Corinthians 12:2)

1662. A thorn in the flesh
(2 Corinthians 12:7)

1663. satan (2 Corinthians 12:7)

1664. Three times (2 Corinthians 12:8)

1665. God's grace (2 Corinthians 12:9)

1666. Through their weakness
(2 Corinthians 12:9)

1667. Signs, wonders, and miracles
(2 Corinthians 12:12)

1668. Two times (2 Corinthians 12:14)

1669. He was afraid there would be
discord, disorder, and sin
(2 Corinthians 12:20-21)

1670. A holy kiss (2 Corinthians 13:12)

Galatians

1671. An angel (Galatians 1:8)

1672. Man (Galatians 1:10)

1673. Judaism (Galatians 1:14)

1674. Arabia (Galatians 1:17)

1675. Three years (Galatians 1:18)

1676. Fifteen days (Galatians 1:18)

1677. James, the brother of Jesus
(Galatians 1:19)

1678. Barnabas and Titus (Galatians 2:1)

1679. Titus (Galatians 2:3)

1680. Cephas/Peter (Galatians 2:7)

1681. James, Cephas/Peter, John
(Galatians 2:9)

1682. Cephas/Peter (Galatians 2:11)

1683. Antioch (Galatians 2:11)

1684. Peter (Galatians 2:12)

1685. Barnabas (Galatians 2:13)

1686. The law (Galatians 2:19)

1687. Righteousness (Galatians 2:21)

1688. Faith (Galatians 3:7)

1689. Faith (Galatians 3:12)

1690. Tree/pole (Galatians 3:13)

1691. 430 years (Galatians 3:17)

1692. The law (Galatians 3:23)

1693. Male and female (Galatians 3:28)

1694. An heir (Galatians 4:7)

1695. An illness (Galatians 4:13)

1696. Abraham (Galatians 4:21-28)

1697. Hagar (Galatians 4:25)

1698. The free woman (Galatians 4:31)

1699. Christ (Galatians 5:2)

1700. Law (Galatians 5:3)

1701. Yeast (Galatians 5:9)

1702. The kingdom of God
(Galatians 5:21)

1703. Love, joy, peace, patience, kindness,
goodness, faithfulness, gentleness,
self-control (Galatians 5:22)

1704. Gently (Galatians 6:1)

1705. Burdens (Galatians 6:2)

1706. Good (Galatians 6:9)

1707. The family of believers
(Galatians 6:10)

1708. Large letters (Galatians 6:11)

1709. The cross of Christ (Galatians 6:14)

1710. The marks of Jesus
(Galatians 6:17)

Ephesians

1711. Holy and blameless
(Ephesians 1:4)

1712. Adoption to sonship
(Ephesians 1:5)

1713. A seal (Ephesians 1:13)

1714. The Holy Spirit (Ephesians 1:13)

1715. Our inheritance (Ephesians 1:14)

1716. His feet (Ephesians 1:22)

1717. The church (Ephesians 1:22)

1718. Our transgressions/sins (Ephesians 2:5)

1719. His grace (Ephesians 2:5)

1720. Boast (Ephesians 2:9)

1721. Good works (Ephesians 2:10)

1722. The blood of Christ (Ephesians 2:13)

1723. Peace (Ephesians 2:17)

1724. Foreigners and aliens (Ephesians 2:19)

1725. Apostles and prophets (Ephesians 2:20)

1726. The cornerstone (Ephesians 2:20)

1727. The Gentiles (Ephesians 3:6)

1728. With freedom and confidence (Ephesians 3:12)

1729. The love of Christ (Ephesians 3:18)

1730. Immeasurably more (Ephesians 3:20)

1731. One body, one spirit, one hope, one Lord, one faith, one baptism, one God and Father (Ephesians 4:5-6)

1732. The waves and winds of earthly teachings (Ephesians 4:14)

1733. Christ (Ephesians 4:15)

1734. Gentiles (Ephesians 4:17)

1735. Self, self (Ephesians 4:22-24)

1736. Their anger (Ephesians 4:26)

1737. The devil (Ephesians 4:27)

1738. Unwholesome (Ephesians 4:29)

1739. The Holy Spirit of God (Ephesians 4:30)

1740. Thanksgiving (Ephesians 5:4)

1741. Evil (Ephesians 5:16)

1742. The Spirit (Ephesians 5:18)

1743. The church (Ephesians 5:23)

1744. Their own bodies (Ephesians 5:28)

1745. One body/flesh (Ephesians 5:31)

1746. Respect (Ephesians 5:33)

1747. Honor your mother and father (Ephesians 6:1)

1748. Their children (Ephesians 6:4)

1749. The devil's (Ephesians 6:11)

1750. Flesh and blood (Ephesians 6:12)

1751. The belt of truth (Ephesians 6:14)

1752. The breastplate (Ephesians 6:14)

1753. Peace (Ephesians 6:15)

1754. The flaming arrows of the evil one (Ephesians 6:16)

1755. Salvation (Ephesians 6:17)

1756. The word of God (Ephesians 6:17)

1757. Chains (Ephesians 6:20)

1758. Tychicus (Ephesians 6:21)

Philippians

1759. Paul and Timothy (Philippians 1:1)

1760. The day of Christ Jesus (Philippians 1:6)

1761. The palace guards (Philippians 1:13)

1762. The brothers and sisters (Philippians 1:14)

1763. Envy, rivalry, goodwill (Philippians 1:15)

1764. Christ was being preached (Philippians 1:18)

1765. Death/dying (Philippians 1:21)

1766. Suffer (Philippians 1:29)

1767. Selfish ambition or vain conceit (Philippians 2:3)

1768. Christ Jesus (Philippians 2:5)

1769. A servant (Philippians 2:7)

1770. A man (Philippians 2:8)

1771. Death on the cross (Philippians 2:8)

1772. Every knee (Philippians 2:10)

1773. Heaven, earth, under earth (Philippians 2:10)

1774. That Jesus Christ is Lord (Philippians 2:11)

1775. Fear and trembling (Philippians 2:12)

1776. Stars in the sky (Philippians 2:15)

1777. A drink offering (Philippians 2:17)

1778. Timothy (Philippians 2:19)

1779. Epaphroditus (Philippians 2:25)

1780. He almost died (Philippians 2:27)

1781. Benjamin (Philippians 3:5)

1782. Pharisee (Philippians 3:5)

1783. A loss/garbage (Philippians 3:7-8)

1784. Resurrection (Philippians 3:10)

1785. Goal, prize (Philippians 3:14)

1786. Their stomach (Philippians 3:19)

1787. Earthly (Philippians 3:19)

1788. Heaven (Philippians 3:20)

1789. Euodia and Synthyche (Philippians 4:2)

1790. Rejoice (Philippians 4:4)

1791. Pray, petition, giving thanks (Philippians 4:6)

1792. The peace of God (Philippians 4:7)

1793. Content (Philippians 4:11)

1794. Strength (Philippians 4:13)

1795. Thessalonica (Philippians 4:16)

1796. Caesar's (Philippians 4:22)

Colossians

1797. Timothy (Colossians 1:1)

1798. The gospel (Colossians 1:6)

1799. Epaphras (Colossians 1:7)

1800. Darkness (Colossians 1:13)

1801. Creation (Colossians 1:15)

1802. The church (Colossians 1:18)

1803. His blood (Colossians 1:20)

1804. Reconciled (Colossians 1:21-22)

1805. The Gentiles (Colossians 1:27)

1806. Laodicea (Colossians 2:1)

1807. In spirit (Colossians 2:5)

1808. Hollow and deceptive (Colossians 2:8)

1809. Human tradition and spiritual forces of the world (Colossians 2:8)

1810. The cross (Colossians 2:14)

1811. The peace of Christ
(Colossians 3:15)

1812. Psalms, hymns and spiritual songs
(Colossians 3:16)

1813. Submit to them (Colossians 3:18)

1814. Love them and don't be harsh
(Colossians 3:19)

1815. Obey them (Colossians 3:20)

1816. Their children (Colossians 3:21)

1817. The Lord (Colossians 3:23)

1818. Salt (Colossians 4:6)

1819. Tychicus (Colossians 4:7)

1820. Onesimus (Colossians 4:9)

1821. Aristarchus (Colossians 4:10)

1822. Mark (Colossians 4:10)

1823. Luke (Colossians 4:14)

1824. Laodicea (Colossians 4:15)

1825. His chains (Colossians 4:18)

1 Thessalonians

1826. Silas and Timothy
(1 Thessalonians 1:1)

1827. Macedonia and Achaia
(1 Thessalonians 1:7)

1828. Philippi (1 Thessalonians 2:2)

1829. People/men (1 Thessalonians 2:4)

1830. satan (1 Thessalonians 2:18)

1831. Athens (1 Thessalonians 3:1)

1832. Timothy (1 Thessalonians 3:2)

1833. Those who had fallen asleep
(1 Thessalonians 4:13)

1834. Hope (1 Thessalonians 4:13)

1835. A trumpet (1 Thessalonians 4:16)

1836. The dead In Christ
(1 Thessalonians 4:16)

1837. Those who are still alive
(1 Thessalonians 4:17)

1838. A thief In the night
(1 Thessalonians 5:2)

1839. The day (1 Thessalonians 5:8)

1840. The breastplate and the helmet
(1 Thessalonians 5:8)

1841. The Spirit (1 Thessalonians 5:19)

1842. Prophecies (1 Thessalonians 5:20)

2 Thessalonians

1843. Paul, Silas, and Timothy
(2 Thessalonians 1:1)

1844. The day of the Lord
(2 Thessalonians 2:2)

1845. God's temple (2 Thessalonians 2:4)

1846. Miracles, signs, and wonders
(2 Thessalonians 2:9)

1847. The truth (2 Thessalonians 2:10)

1848. By word of mouth or by his letters
(2 Thessalonians 2:15)

1849. Work (2 Thessalonians 3:8)

1850. Eat (2 Thessalonians 3:10)

1851. Busy bodies
(2 Thessalonians 3:11)

1 Timothy

1852. Ephesus (1 Timothy 1:3)

1853. Sinners (1 Timothy 1:15)

1854. Hymenaeus and Alexander (1 Timothy 1:19)

1855. satan (1 Timothy 1:20)

1856. Kings and authorities (1 Timothy 2:2)

1857. Holy hands (1 Timothy 2:8)

1858. Modestly (1 Timothy 2:9)

1859. Good deeds (1 Timothy 2:10)

1860. Overseers/elders and deacons (1 Timothy 3:1-13)

1861. His family (1 Timothy 3:5)

1862. His conversion (1 Timothy 3:6)

1863. Outsiders (1 Timothy 3:7)

1864. Wine (1 Timothy 3:8)

1865. Demons (1 Timothy 4:1)

1866. Food (1 Timothy 4:3)

1867. Young (1 Timothy 4:12)

1868. An unbeliever (1 Timothy 5:8)

1869. Sixty (1 Timothy 5:9)

1870. Idle/busybodies (1 Timothy 5:13)

1871. Two or more (1 Timothy 5:19)

1872. Wine (1 Timothy 5:23)

1873. Words (1 Timothy 6:4)

1874. Godliness (1 Timothy 6:5)

1875. Food and clothing (1 Timothy 6:8)

1876. Evil (1 Timothy 6:10)

1877. Griefs (1 Timothy 6:10)

1878. The faith (1 Timothy 6:12)

1879. Pontius Pilate (1 Timothy 6:13)

1880. Good deeds (1 Timothy 6:18)

1881. Knowledge (1 Timothy 6:20)

2 Timothy

1882. Lois (2 Timothy 1:5)

1883. Eunice (2 Timothy 1:5)

1884. Timid (2 Timothy 1:7)

1885. They deserted him (2 Timothy 1:15)

1886. Onesiphorus' (2 Timothy 1:16)

1887. The word of truth (2 Timothy 2:15)

1888. Gangrene (2 Timothy 2:17)

1889. The resurrection (2 Timothy 2:17-18)

1890. Quarrels (2 Timothy 2:23)

1891. Moses (2 Timothy 3:8)

1892. Antioch, Iconium, Lystra (2 Timothy 3:11)

1893. Teaching, rebuking, correcting, training (2 Timothy 3:16)

1894. Every good work (2 Timothy 3:17)

1895. Sound doctrine (2 Timothy 4:3)

1896. Ears (2 Timothy 4:3)

1897. Myths (2 Timothy 4:4)

1898. A drink offering (2 Timothy 4:6)

1899. Fight (2 Timothy 4:7)

1900. The race (2 Timothy 4:7)

1901. A crown of righteousness (2 Timothy 4:8)

1902. Demas (2 Timothy 4:10)

1903. Luke (2 Timothy 4:11)

1904. Mark (2 Timothy 4:11)

1905. His cloak and scrolls/the parchments (2 Timothy 4:13)

1906. Alexander (2 Timothy 4:14)

1907. Priscilla and Aquila (2 Timothy 4:19)

Titus

1908. Crete (Titus 1:5)

1909. Elders (Titus 1:5)

1910. The circumcision group (Titus 1:10)

1911. Cretans (Titus 1:12)

1912. Their actions (Titus 1:16)

1913. Older men (Titus 2:2)

1914. Older women (Titus 2:3)

1915. Wine (Titus 2:3)

1916. Younger women (Titus 2:4-5)

1917. Younger men (Titus 2:6-7)

1918. Slaves (Titus 2:9)

1919. The Holy Spirit (Titus 3:5)

1920. Twice (Titus 3:10)

1921. Nicopolis (Titus 3:12)

1922. A lawyer (Titus 3:13)

Philemon

1923. Timothy (Philemon 1)

1924. Apphia and Archippus (Philemon 2)

1925. Paul was in chains (Philemon 10)

1926. A brother (Philemon 16)

1927. He offered to pay for them himself (Philemon 18)

1928. His very self (Philemon 19)

1929. A guest room (Philemon 22)

1930. Epaphras (Philemon 23)

1931. Mark and Luke (Philemon 24)

Hebrews

1932. The Son/Jesus (Hebrews 1:3)

1933. Angels (Hebrews 1:4)

1934. The heavens and the earth (Hebrews 1:10-12)

1935. Angels (Hebrews 2:9)

1936. The devil (Hebrews 2:14)

1937. Moses (Hebrews 3:5-6)

1938. Encourage one another (Hebrews 3:13)

1939. A double-edged sword (Hebrews 4:12)

1940. Soul, spirit, joints, marrow (Hebrews 4:12)

1941. Our weaknesses (Hebrews 4:15)

1942. Sin (Hebrews 4:15)

1943. Melchizedek's (Hebrews 5:10)

1944. Solid food (Hebrews 5:12)

1945. Himself (Hebrews 6:13)

1946. Lie (Hebrews 6:18)

1947. Melchizedek (Hebrews 7:1)

1948. King of righteousness (Hebrews 7:2)

1949. King of peace (Hebrews 7:2)

1950. Father/mother/parent, genealogy, beginning of days/birthday, end of life/death day (Hebrews 7:3)

1951. Levi (Hebrews 7:6)

1952. Aaronic (Hebrews 7:11)

1953. Judah (Hebrews 7:14)

1954. A sanctuary (Hebrews 8:5)

1955. A new covenant (Hebrews 8:6-7, 13)

1956. The gold jar of manna, Aaron's staff that budded, and the stone tablets of the covenant (Hebrews 9:4)

1957. The inner room/the Most Holy Place (Hebrews 9:7)

1958. Goats and calves (Hebrews 9:12)

1959. Blood (Hebrews 9:22)

1960. Forgiveness (Hebrews 9:22)

1961. Once (Hebrews 9:27)

1962. The law (Hebrews 10:1)

1963. Sins (Hebrews 10:4)

1964. Meeting together (Hebrews 10:25)

1965. See (Hebrews 11:1)

1966. Enoch (Hebrews 11:5)

1967. Faith (Hebrews 11:6)

1968. God exists and he rewards those who seek him (Hebrews 11:6)

1969. God's city (Hebrews 11:9-10)

1970. Sarah (Hebrews 11:11)

1971. A heavenly country (Hebrews 11:16)

1972. Pharaoh's daughter (Hebrews 11:24)

1973. Gideon, Barak, Samson, Jephthah (Hebrews 11:32)

1974. David (Hebrews 11:32)

1975. A great cloud of witnesses (Hebrews 12:1)

1976. His children (Hebrews 12:7)

1977. Discipline (Hebrews 12:11)

1978. A kingdom (Hebrews 12:28)

1979. Angels (Hebrews 13:2)

1980. The marriage bed (Hebrews 13:4)

1981. Jesus Christ (Hebrews 13:8)

1982. Timothy (Hebrews 13:23)

1983. Italy (Hebrews 13:24)

James

1984. The twelve tribes scattered (James 1:1)

1985. When they face trials (James 1:2)

1986. Perseverance (James 1:3)

1987. Wisdom (James 1:5)

1988. A wave of the sea, tossed by wind (James 1:6)

1989. The rich (James 1:10-11)

1990. The crown of life (James 1:12)

1991. God (James 1:13)

1992. Listen (James 1:19)

1993. To speak and to get angry (James 1:19)

1994. The word (James 1:21)

1995. A mirror (James 1:23)

1996. Orphans and widows (James 1:27)

1997. A seat (James 2:3)

1998. Faith (James 2:5)

1999. Mercy (James 2:13)

2000. Faith (James 2:17)

2001. Demons (James 2:19)

2002. Abraham and Rahab (James 2:21, 25)

2003. A teacher (James 3:1)

2004. Horse (James 3:3)

2005. Rudder (James 3:4)

2006. A forest (James 3:5)

2007. Tame it (James 3:7-8)

2008. Poison (James 3:8)

2009. Fresh and salt (James 3:11)

2010. Ask God (James 4:2)

2011. Motives (James 4:3)

2012. The world (James 4:4)

2013. The devil (James 4:7)

2014. Job (James 5:11)

2015. Oil (James 5:14)

2016. A righteous person (James 5:16)

2017. Elijah (James 5:17)

1 Peter

2018. In heaven (1 Peter 1:4)

2019. The salvation of our souls (1 Peter 1:9)

2020. Because God is holy (1 Peter 1:14-15)

2021. Silver or gold (1 Peter 1:18)

2022. Pure spiritual milk (1 Peter 2:2)

2023. Stones (1 Peter 2:5)

2024. Priesthood (1 Peter 2:9)

2025. Good deeds (1 Peter 2:12)

2026. Insults (1 Peter 2:23)

2027. Wounds (1 Peter 2:24)

2028. A gentle and quiet spirit (1 Peter 3:4)

2029. By being submissive to their husbands (1 Peter 3:4)

2030. Sarah (1 Peter 3:6)

2031. Hope (1 Peter 3:15)

2032. In prison (1 Peter 3:19)

2033. Noah (1 Peter 3:20)

2034. Baptism (1 Peter 3:20-21)

2035. Love (1 Peter 4:8)

2036. A Christian (1 Peter 4:16)

2037. The crown of glory (1 Peter 5:4)

2038. Our anxiety (1 Peter 5:7)

2039. Lion (1 Peter 5:8)

2040. Silas and Mark (1 Peter 5:12-13)

2 Peter

2041. On that sacred mountain (2 Peter 1:17-18)

2042. Interpretation (2 Peter 1:20)

2043. Noah (2 Peter 2:5)

2044. Lot (2 Peter 2:7-8)

2045. Balaam's donkey (2 Peter 2:15-16)

2046. Freedom (2 Peter 2:19)

2047. A thousand (2 Peter 3:8)

2048. Repentance (2 Peter 3:9)

2049. A thief (2 Peter 3:10)

2050. Holy and godly (2 Peter 3:11-12)

2051. Paul's (2 Peter 3:15-16)

1 John

2052. Hearing, seeing, touching (1 John 1:1)

2053. His joy (1 John 1:4)

2054. Darkness (1 John 1:5)

2055. Fellowship (1 John 1:7)

2056. Forgive our sins and purify us from unrighteousness (1 John 1:9)

2057. A liar (1 John 1:10)

2058. His commands (1 John 2:3)

2059. Darkness (1 John 2:11)

2060. The lust of the flesh, the lust of the eyes, the pride of life (1 John 2:16)

2061. Antichrists (1 John 2:18)

2062. The Father and the Son (1 John 2:22)

2063. The devil (1 John 3:8)

2064. The devil's work (1 John 3:8)

2065. The world (1 John 3:13)

2066. A murderer (1 John 3:15)

2067. He laid down his life (1 John 3:16)

2068. Actions and in truth (1 John 3:18)

2069. The spirits (1 John 4:1)

2070. That Jesus Christ came in the flesh (1 John 4:2)

2071. The world (1 John 4:4)

2072. He sent his one and only Son (1 John 4:9)

2073. Fear (1 John 4:18)

2074. Punishment (1 John 4:18)

2075. God (1 John 4:19)

2076. A liar (1 John 4:20)

2077. His commands (1 John 5:2)

2078. Water and blood (1 John 5:6)

2079. The Spirit, the water, the blood (1 John 5:7-8)

2080. Life (1 John 5:11)

2081. Idols (1 John 5:21)

2 John

2082. The elder (2 John 1)

2083. The chosen lady and her children (2 John 1)

2084. Jesus has come in the flesh (2 John 7)

2085. With paper and ink (2 John 12)

2086. Visit them face to face (2 John 12)

3 John

2087. The elder (3 John 1)

2088. Gaius (3 John 1)

2089. Diotrephes (3 John 9)

2090. Demetrius (3 John 12)

2091. Pen and ink (3 John 13)

Jude

2092. James (Jude 1)

2093. Ungodly people who deny Christ (Jude 4)

2094. In darkness, bound with everlasting chains (Jude 6)

2095. Sodom and Gomorrah (Jude 7)

2096. Michael (Jude 9)

2097. Moses' (Jude 9)

2098. Cain, Balaam, Korah (Jude 11)

2099. Enoch (Jude 14)

2100. The fire (Jude 23)

Revelation

2101. An angel (Revelation 1:1)

2102. Seven churches (Revelation 1:4)

2103. Asia (Revelation 1:4)

2104. Pierced him (Revelation 1:7)

2105. Omega (Revelation 1:8)

2106. Patmos (Revelation 1:9)

2107. Seven lampstands (Revelation 1:12)

2108. A son of man (Revelation 1:13)

2109. Wool (Revelation 1:14)

2110. A furnace (Revelation 1:15)

2111. Seven stars (Revelation 1:16)

2112. Sharp double-edged sword (Revelation 1:16)

2113. Death and Hades (Revelation 1:18)

2114. Angels of the seven churches (Revelation 1:20)

2115. The seven churches (Revelation 1:20)

2116. Seven stars (Revelation 2:1)

2117. The right hand (Revelation 2:1)

2118. Seven lampstands (Revelation 2:1)

2119. Wicked men (Revelation 2:2)

2120. Apostles (Revelation 2:2)

2121. Their first love (Revelation 2:4)

2122. Their lampstand (Revelation 2:5)

2123. The Nicolatians (Revelation 2:6)

2124. The tree of life (Revelation 2:7)

2125. Smyrna (Revelation 2:9)

2126. The synagogue of satan (Revelation 2:9)

2127. Ten days (Revelation 2:10)

2128. satan (Revelation 2:13)

2129. Antipas (Revelation 2:13)

2130. Balaam and Nicolatians (Revelation 2:14-15)

2131. White stone (Revelation 2:17)

2132. Jezebel (Revelation 2:20)

2133. Sexual immorality and eating food sacrificed to idols (Revelation 2:20)

2134. Being alive, but dead (Revelation 3:1)

2135. Thief (Revelation 3:3)

2136. Their clothes (Revelation 3:4)

2137. David (Revelation 3:7)

2138. A door (Revelation 3:8)

2139. satan (Revelation 3:9)

2140. Their crown (Revelation 3:11)

2141. The temple of God (Revelation 3:12)

2142. Hot nor cold (Revelation 3:15-16)

2143. Lukewarm (Revelation 3:16)

2144. Salve (Revelation 3:18)

2145. Eat with them (Revelation 3:20)

2146. A trumpet (Revelation 4:1)

2147. A rainbow (Revelation 4:3)

2148. Twenty-four thrones (Revelation 4:4)

2149. Elders (Revelation 4:4)

2150. Crowns of gold (Revelation 4:4)

2151. Seven lamps (Revelation 4:5)

2152. The seven spirits of God (Revelation 4:5)

2153. Four living creatures (Revelation 4:6)

2154. Eyes (Revelation 4:6)

2155. A lion, ox, man, flying eagle (Revelation 4:7)

2156. Six wings (Revelation 4:8)

2157. Their crowns (Revelation 4:10)

2158. Seven seals (Revelation 5:1)

2159. The lion of the tribe of Judah, the root of David, the Lamb (Revelation 5:5-6)

2160. Seven horns and seven eyes (Revelation 5:6)

2161. Harps and golden bowls of incense (Revelation 5:8)

2162. The prayers of the people (Revelation 5:8)

2163. Angels (Revelation 5:11)

2164. White, red, black, pale (Revelation 6:1-8)

2165. A bow (Revelation 6:2)

2166. A large sword (Revelation 6:4)

2167. Scales (Revelation 6:5)

2168. Death (Revelation 6:8)

2169. Hades (Revelation 6:8)

2170. Sword, famine, plague, wild beasts (Revelation 6:8)

2171. White robes (Revelation 6:11)

2172. Black (Revelation 6:12)

2173. Red (Revelation 6:12)

2174. Earth, sun, moon, stars (Revelation 6:12-14)

2175. In caves and the rocks of mountains (Revelation 6:15)

2176. 144,000 (Revelation 7:4)

2177. 12,000 each (Revelation 7:5-8)

2178. Palm branches (Revelation 7:9)

2179. The great tribulation (Revelation 7:14)

2180. The blood of the lamb (Revelation 7:14)

2181. Half an hour (Revelation 8:1)

2182. Seven trumpets (Revelation 8:2)

2183. A censer filled with fire (Revelation 8:5)

2184. Hail and fire mixed with blood (Revelation 8:7)

2185. The sea (Revelation 8:8)

2186. A great star (Revelation 8:10)

2187. Wormwood (Revelation 8:11)

2188. Bitter (Revelation 8:11)

2189. Sun, moon, stars (Revelation 8:12)

2190. An eagle (Revelation 8:13)

2191. A star (Revelation 9:1)

2192. Locusts (Revelation 9:3)

2193. Five months (Revelation 9:5)

2194. A scorpion (Revelation 9:5)

2195. Abaddon (Revelation 9:11)

2196. Apollyon (Revelation 9:11)

2197. Euphrates (Revelation 9:14)

2198. One third (Revelation 9:15)

2199. Fire, smoke, sulfur (Revelation 9:18)

2200. Snakes (Revelation 9:19)

2201. A scroll (Revelation 10:2)

2202. The sea and dry land (Revelation 10:2)

2203. Seven thunders (Revelation 10:3-4)

2204. Sweet (Revelation 10:10)

2205. Sour (Revelation 10:10)

2206. A measuring rod (Revelation 11:1)

2207. The temple (Revelation 11:1)

2208. Forty-two months (Revelation 11:2)

2209. 1,260 days (Revelation 11:3)

2210. Fire (Revelation 11:5)

2211. The beast (Revelation 11:7)

2212. Sodom and Egypt (Revelation 11:8)

2213. Three and a half days (Revelation 11:9-10)

2214. By giving each other gifts (Revelation 11:10)

2215. An earthquake (Revelation 11:13)

2216. Seven thousand people (Revelation 11:13)

2217. The sun, moon, and stars (Revelation 12:1)

2218. Seven heads, ten horns, seven crowns (Revelation 12:3)

2219. One-third (Revelation 12:4)

2220. A son/a male child (Revelation 12:5)

2221. 1,260 days (Revelation 12:6)

2222. Michael (Revelation 12:7)

2223. The devil and satan (Revelation 12:9)

2224. Eagle (Revelation 12:14)

2225. Leopard, bear, lion (Revelation 13:2)

2226. A fatal wound (Revelation 13:3)

2227. It had been healed (Revelation 13:3)

2228. The beast (Revelation 13:4)

2229. Forty-two months (Revelation 13:5)

2230. A lamb (Revelation 13:11)

2231. A dragon (Revelation 13:11)

2232. They were killed (Revelation 13:15)

2233. On the right hand and forehead (Revelation 13:16)

2234. Buy or sell (Revelation 13:17)

2235. 666 (Revelation 13:18)

2236. Mount Zion (Revelation 14:1)

2237. Women (Revelation 14:4)

2238. Babylon (Revelation 14:8)

2239. The wine of her adulteries (Revelation 14:8)

2240. A sickle (Revelation 14:15)

2241. To the horses' bridle (Revelation 14:20)

2242. Plagues (Revelation 15:6)

2243. Seven golden bowls (Revelation 15:7)

2244. Ugly and painful sores (Revelation 16:2)

2245. Blood (Revelation 16:3)

2246. Blood (Revelation 16:4)

2247. The sun (Revelation 16:8)

2248. Darkness (Revelation 16:10)

2249. The Euphrates (Revelation 16:12)

2250. Frogs (Revelation 16:13)

2251. The dragon, the first beast, the false prophet (Revelation 16:13)

2252. Armageddon (Revelation 16:16)

2253. An earthquake (Revelation 16:18)

2254. Three sections (Revelation 16:19)

2255. About one hundred pounds (Revelation 16:21)

2256. The kings of the earth (Revelation 17:2)

2257. Scarlet (Revelation 17:3)

2258. Blasphemous names (Revelation 17:3)

2259. Seven heads and ten horns (Revelation 17:3)

2260. Purple, scarlet, gold (Revelation 17:3,4)

2261. A golden cup (Revelation 17:4)

2262. The saints' blood/God's people (Revelation 17:6)

2263. Kings (Revelation 17:10,12)

2264. The people, multitude, nations, languages (Revelation 17:15)

2265. The great city that rules over the kings of the earth (Revelation 17:18)

2266. Babylon the Great (Revelation 18:2)

2267. Kings, merchants and ship captains/sailors (Revelation 18:9,11,17)

2268. A boulder (Revelation 18:21)

2269. The righteous acts of the saints (Revelation 19:8)

2270. Faithful and true (Revelation 19:11)

2271. Blood (Revelation 19:13)

2272. A sharp sword (Revelation 19:15)

2273. The false prophet (Revelation 19:20)

2274. The fiery lake of burning sulfur (Revelation 19:20)

2275. Birds (Revelation 19:21)

2276. The key to the Abyss and a great chain (Revelation 20:1)

2277. That ancient serpent, the devil, satan (Revelation 20:2)

2278. A thousand years (Revelation 20:2)

2279. Beheaded (Revelation 20:4)

2280. The beast and his image (Revelation 20:4)

2281. Gog and Magog (Revelation 20:8)

2282. The beast and the false prophet (Revelation 20:10)

2283. Books (Revelation 20:12)

2284. The second death (Revelation 20:14)

2285. The lake of fire (Revelation 20:15)

2286. A sea (Revelation 21:1)

2287. Tears (Revelation 21:4)

2288. Death, mourning, crying, pain (Revelation 21:4)

2289. The Alpha and Omega (Revelation 21:6)

2290. In the fiery lake of burning sulfur (Revelation 21:8)

2291. Twelve gates (Revelation 21:12)

2292. The twelve tribes of Israel (Revelation 21:12)

2293. Three gates in four directions (Revelation 21:13)

2294. The names of the twelve apostles (Revelation 21:14)

2295. A measuring rod of gold (Revelation 21:15)

2296. A square (Revelation 21:16)

2297. Twelve types of stones (Revelation 21:19-20)

2298. Pearl (Revelation 21:21)

2299. Gold (Revelation 21:21)

2300. A temple (Revelation 21:22)

2301. Sun or moon (Revelation 21:23)

2302. The Lamb's book of life (Revelation 21:27)

2303. The river of the water of life (Revelation 22:1-2)

2304. The tree of life (Revelation 22:2)

2305. Twelve crops (Revelation 22:2)

2306. The nations (Revelation 22:2)

2307. Night (Revelation 22:5)

2308. Three times
(Revelation 22:7,12,20)

2309. Alpha, Last, Beginning
(Revelation 22:13)

2310. Wash them (Revelation 22:14)

2311. Dogs (Revelation 22:15)

2312. David (Revelation 22:16)

2313. Bright morning star
(Revelation 22:16)

2314. "Come" (Revelation 22:17)

2315. The water of life (Revelation 22:17)

2316. Amen (Revelation 22:21)

Keep Score

Which questions did you answer correctly?
Make copies and challenge your friends!

Question #	✔	Question #	✔	Question #	✔	Question #	✔	Question #	✔
Matthew		25		50		75		100	
1		26		51		76		101	
2		27		52		77		102	
3		28		53		78		103	
4		29		54		79		104	
5		30		55		80		105	
6		31		56		81		106	
7		32		57		82		107	
8		33		58		83		108	
9		34		59		84		109	
10		35		60		85		110	
11		36		61		86		111	
12		37		62		87		112	
13		38		63		88		113	
14		39		64		89		114	
15		40		65		90		115	
16		41		66		91		116	
17		42		67		92		117	
18		43		68		93		118	
19		44		69		94		119	
20		45		70		95		120	
21		46		71		96		121	
22		47		72		97		122	
23		48		73		98		123	
24		49		74		99		124	

Question #	✔	Question #	✔	Question #	✔	Question #	✔	Question #	✔
125		157		189		221		253	
126		158		190		222		254	
127		159		191		223		255	
128		160		192		224		256	
129		161		193		225		257	
130		162		194		226		258	
131		163		195		227		259	
132		164		196		228		260	
133		165		197		229		261	
134		166		198		230		262	
135		167		199		231		263	
136		168		200		232		264	
137		169		201		233		265	
138		170		202		234		266	
139		171		203		235		267	
140		172		204		236		268	
141		173		205		237		269	
142		174		206		238		270	
143		175		207		239		271	
144		176		208		240		272	
145		177		209		241		273	
146		178		210		242		274	
147		179		211		243		275	
148		180		212		244		276	
149		181		213		245		277	
150		182		214		246		278	
151		183		215		247		279	
152		184		216		248		280	
153		185		217		249		281	
154		186		218		250		282	
155		187		219		251		283	
156		188		220		252		284	

Question #	✔	Question #	✔	Question #	✔	Question #	✔	Question #	✔
285		317		349		380		412	
286		318		350		381		413	
287		319		351		382		414	
288		320		352		383		415	
289		321		353		384		416	
290		322		354		385		417	
291		323		355		386		418	
292		324		356		387		419	
293		325		357		388		420	
294		326		358		389		421	
295		327		359		390		422	
296		328		360		391		423	
297		329		361		392		424	
298		330		362		393		425	
299		331		363		394		426	
300		332		364		395		427	
301		333		365		396		428	
302		334		366		397		429	
303		335		367		398		430	
304		336		368		399		431	
305		337		369		400		432	
306		338		Mark		401		433	
307		339		370		402		434	
308		340		371		403		435	
309		341		372		404		436	
310		342		373		405		437	
311		343		374		406		438	
312		344		375		407		439	
313		345		376		408		440	
314		346		377		409		441	
315		347		378		410		442	
316		348		379		411		443	

Question #	✔	Question #	✔	Question #	✔	Question #	✔	Question #	✔
444		476		508		540		572	
445		477		509		541		573	
446		478		510		542		574	
447		479		511		543		575	
448		480		512		544		576	
449		481		513		545		577	
450		482		514		546		578	
451		483		515		547		*Luke*	
452		484		516		548		579	
453		485		517		549		580	
454		486		518		550		581	
455		487		519		551		582	
456		488		520		552		583	
457		489		521		553		584	
458		490		522		554		585	
459		491		523		555		586	
460		492		524		556		587	
461		493		525		557		588	
462		494		526		558		589	
463		495		527		559		590	
464		496		528		560		591	
465		497		529		561		592	
466		498		530		562		593	
467		499		531		563		594	
468		500		532		564		595	
469		501		533		565		596	
470		502		534		566		597	
471		503		535		567		598	
472		504		536		568		599	
473		505		537		569		600	
474		506		538		570		601	
475		507		539		571		602	

Question #	✔	Question #	✔	Question #	✔	Question #	✔	Question #	✔
603		635		667		699		731	
604		636		668		700		732	
605		637		669		701		733	
606		638		670		702		734	
607		639		671		703		735	
608		640		672		704		736	
609		641		673		705		737	
610		642		674		706		738	
611		643		675		707		739	
612		644		676		708		740	
613		645		677		709		741	
614		646		678		710		742	
615		647		679		711		743	
616		648		680		712		744	
617		649		681		713		745	
618		650		682		714		746	
619		651		683		715		747	
620		652		684		716		748	
621		653		685		717		749	
622		654		686		718		750	
623		655		687		719		751	
624		656		688		720		752	
625		657		689		721		753	
626		658		690		722		754	
627		659		691		723		755	
628		660		692		724		756	
629		661		693		725		757	
630		662		694		726		758	
631		663		695		727		759	
632		664		696		728		760	
633		665		697		729		761	
634		666		698		730		762	

Question #	✔	Question #	✔	Question #	✔	Question #	✔	Question #	✔
763		795		827		859		891	
764		796		828		860		892	
765		797		829		861		893	
766		798		830		862		894	
767		799		831		863		895	
768		800		832		864		896	
769		801		833		865		897	
770		802		834		866		898	
771		803		835		867		899	
772		804		836		868		900	
773		805		837		869		901	
774		806		838		870		902	
775		807		839		871		903	
776		808		840		872		904	
777		809		841		873		905	
778		810		842		874		906	
779		811		843		875		907	
780		812		844		876		908	
781		813		845		877		909	
782		814		846		878		910	
783		815		847		879		911	
784		816		848		880		912	
785		817		849		881		913	
786		818		850		882		914	
787		819		851		883		915	
788		820		852		884		916	
789		821		853		885		917	
790		822		854		886		918	
791		823		855		887		919	
792		824		856		888		920	
793		825		857		889		921	
794		826		858		890		922	

Question #	✔	Question #	✔	Question #	✔	Question #	✔	Question #	✔
923		954		986		1018		1050	
John		955		987		1019		1051	
924		956		988		1020		1052	
925		957		989		1021		1053	
926		958		990		1022		1054	
927		959		991		1023		1055	
928		960		992		1024		1056	
929		961		993		1025		1057	
930		962		994		1026		1058	
931		963		995		1027		1059	
932		964		996		1028		1060	
933		965		997		1029		1061	
934		966		998		1030		1062	
935		967		999		1031		1063	
936		968		1000		1032		1064	
937		969		1001		1033		1065	
938		970		1002		1034		1066	
939		971		1003		1035		1067	
940		972		1004		1036		1068	
941		973		1005		1037		1069	
942		974		1006		1038		1070	
943		975		1007		1039		1071	
944		976		1008		1040		1072	
945		977		1009		1041		1073	
946		978		1010		1042		1074	
947		979		1011		1043		1075	
948		980		1012		1044		1076	
949		981		1013		1045		1077	
950		982		1014		1046		1078	
951		983		1015		1047		1079	
952		984		1016		1048		1080	
953		985		1017		1049		1081	

Question #	✔	Question #	✔	Question #	✔	Question #	✔	Question #	✔
1082		1114		1146		1177		1209	
1083		1115		1147		1178		1210	
1084		1116		1148		1179		1211	
1085		1117		1149		1180		1212	
1086		1118		1150		1181		1213	
1087		1119		1151		1182		1214	
1088		1120		1152		1183		1215	
1089		1121		1153		1184		1216	
1090		1122		*Acts*		1185		1217	
1091		1123		1154		1186		1218	
1092		1124		1155		1187		1219	
1093		1125		1156		1188		1220	
1094		1126		1157		1189		1221	
1095		1127		1158		1190		1222	
1096		1128		1159		1191		1223	
1097		1129		1160		1192		1224	
1098		1130		1161		1193		1225	
1099		1131		1162		1194		1226	
1100		1132		1163		1195		1227	
1101		1133		1164		1196		1228	
1102		1134		1165		1197		1229	
1103		1135		1166		1198		1230	
1104		1136		1167		1199		1231	
1105		1137		1168		1200		1232	
1106		1138		1169		1201		1233	
1107		1139		1170		1202		1234	
1108		1140		1171		1203		1235	
1109		1141		1172		1204		1236	
1110		1142		1173		1205		1237	
1111		1143		1174		1206		1238	
1112		1144		1175		1207		1239	
1113		1145		1176		1208		1240	

Question #	✔	Question #	✔	Question #	✔	Question #	✔	Question #	✔
1241		1273		1305		1337		1369	
1242		1274		1306		1338		1370	
1243		1275		1307		1339		1371	
1244		1276		1308		1340		1372	
1245		1277		1309		1341		1373	
1246		1278		1310		1342		1374	
1247		1279		1311		1343		1375	
1248		1280		1312		1344		1376	
1249		1281		1313		1345		1377	
1250		1282		1314		1346		1378	
1251		1283		1315		1347		1379	
1252		1284		1316		1348		1380	
1253		1285		1317		1349		1381	
1254		1286		1318		1350		1382	
1255		1287		1319		1351		1383	
1256		1288		1320		1352		1384	
1257		1289		1321		1353		1385	
1258		1290		1322		1354		1386	
1259		1291		1323		1355		1387	
1260		1292		1324		1356		1388	
1261		1293		1325		1357		1389	
1262		1294		1326		1358		1390	
1263		1295		1327		1359		1391	
1264		1296		1328		1360		1392	
1265		1297		1329		1361		1393	
1266		1298		1330		1362		1394	
1267		1299		1331		1363		1395	
1268		1300		1332		1364		1396	
1269		1301		1333		1365		1397	
1270		1302		1334		1366		1398	
1271		1303		1335		1367		1399	
1272		1304		1336		1368		Romans	

Question #	✔	Question #	✔	Question #	✔	Question #	✔	Question #	✔
1400		1432		1464		1496		1527	
1401		1433		1465		1497		1528	
1402		1434		1466		1498		1529	
1403		1435		1467		1499		1530	
1404		1436		1468		1500		1531	
1405		1437		1469		1501		1532	
1406		1438		1470		1502		1533	
1407		1439		1471		1503		1534	
1408		1440		1472		1504		1535	
1409		1441		1473		1505		1536	
1410		1442		1474		1506		1537	
1411		1443		1475		1507		1538	
1412		1444		1476		1508		1539	
1413		1445		1477		1509		1540	
1414		1446		1478		1510		1541	
1415		1447		1479		1511		1542	
1416		1448		1480		1512		1543	
1417		1449		1481		1513		1544	
1418		1450		1482		1 Corinthians		1545	
1419		1451		1483		1514		1546	
1420		1452		1484		1515		1547	
1421		1453		1485		1516		1548	
1422		1454		1486		1517		1549	
1423		1455		1487		1518		1550	
1424		1456		1488		1519		1551	
1425		1457		1489		1520		1552	
1426		1458		1490		1521		1553	
1427		1459		1491		1522		1554	
1428		1460		1492		1523		1555	
1429		1461		1493		1524		1556	
1430		1462		1494		1525		1557	
1431		1463		1495		1526		1558	

Question #	✔	Question #	✔	Question #	✔	Question #	✔	Question #	✔
1559		1591		1622		1654		1685	
1560		1592		1623		1655		1686	
1561		1593		1624		1656		1687	
1562		1594		1625		1657		1688	
1563		1595		1626		1658		1689	
1564		1596		1627		1659		1690	
1565		1597		1628		1660		1691	
1566		1598		1629		1661		1692	
1567		1599		1630		1662		1693	
1568		1600		1631		1663		1694	
1569		1601		1632		1664		1695	
1570		1602		1633		1665		1696	
1571		1603		1634		1666		1697	
1572		1604		1635		1667		1698	
1573		1605		1636		1668		1699	
1574		1606		1637		1669		1700	
1575		1607		1638		1670		1701	
1576		1608		1639		*Galatians*		1702	
1577		1609		1640		1671		1703	
1578		1610		1641		1672		1704	
1579		1611		1642		1673		1705	
1580		1612		1643		1674		1706	
1581		1613		1644		1675		1707	
1582		1614		1645		1676		1708	
1583		1615		1646		1677		1709	
1584		1616		1647		1678		1710	
1585		1617		1648		1679		*Ephesians*	
1586		1618		1649		1680		1711	
1587		1619		1650		1681		1712	
1588		1620		1651		1682		1713	
1589		*2 Corinthians*		1652		1683		1714	
1590		1621		1653		1684		1715	

KEEP SCORE

Question #	✔	Question #	✔	Question #	✔	Question #	✔	Question #	✔
1716		1748		1779		1810		1841	
1717		1749		1780		1811		1842	
1718		1750		1781		1812		2 Thessalonians	
1719		1751		1782		1813		1843	
1720		1752		1783		1814		1844	
1721		1753		1784		1815		1845	
1722		1754		1785		1816		1846	
1723		1755		1786		1817		1847	
1724		1756		1787		1818		1848	
1725		1757		1788		1819		1849	
1726		1758		1789		1820		1850	
1727		Philippians		1790		1821		1851	
1728		1759		1791		1822		1 Timothy	
1729		1760		1792		1823		1852	
1730		1761		1793		1824		1853	
1731		1762		1794		1825		1854	
1732		1763		1795		1 Thessalonians		1855	
1733		1764		1796		1826		1856	
1734		1765		Colossians		1827		1857	
1735		1766		1797		1828		1858	
1736		1767		1798		1829		1859	
1737		1768		1799		1830		1860	
1738		1769		1800		1831		1861	
1739		1770		1801		1832		1862	
1740		1771		1802		1833		1863	
1741		1772		1803		1834		1864	
1742		1773		1804		1835		1865	
1743		1774		1805		1836		1866	
1744		1775		1806		1837		1867	
1745		1776		1807		1838		1868	
1746		1777		1808		1839		1869	
1747		1778		1809		1840		1870	

Question #	✔	Question #	✔	Question #	✔	Question #	✔	Question #	✔
1871		1902		*Hebrews*		1963		1994	
1872		1903		1932		1964		1995	
1873		1904		1933		1965		1996	
1874		1905		1934		1966		1997	
1875		1906		1935		1967		1998	
1876		1907		1936		1968		1999	
1877		*Titus*		1937		1969		2000	
1878		1908		1938		1970		2001	
1879		1909		1939		1971		2002	
1880		1910		1940		1972		2003	
1881		1911		1941		1973		2004	
2 Timothy		1912		1942		1974		2005	
1882		1913		1943		1975		2006	
1883		1914		1944		1976		2007	
1884		1915		1945		1977		2008	
1885		1916		1946		1978		2009	
1886		1917		1947		1979		2010	
1887		1918		1948		1980		2011	
1888		1919		1949		1981		2012	
1889		1920		1950		1982		2013	
1890		1921		1951		1983		2014	
1891		1922		1952		*James*		2015	
1892		*Philemon*		1953		1984		2016	
1893		1923		1954		1985		2017	
1894		1924		1955		1986		*1 Peter*	
1895		1925		1956		1987		2018	
1896		1926		1957		1988		2019	
1897		1927		1958		1989		2020	
1898		1928		1959		1990		2021	
1899		1929		1960		1991		2022	
1900		1930		1961		1992		2023	
1901		1931		1962		1993		2024	

Question #	✔	Question #	✔	Question #	✔	Question #	✔	Question #	✔
2025		2055		2086		2115		2147	
2026		2056		*3 John*		2116		2148	
2027		2057		2087		2117		2149	
2028		2058		2088		2118		2150	
2029		2059		2089		2119		2151	
2030		2060		2090		2120		2152	
2031		2061		2091		2121		2153	
2032		2062		*Jude*		2122		2154	
2033		2063		2092		2123		2155	
2034		2064		2093		2124		2156	
2035		2065		2094		2125		2157	
2036		2066		2095		2126		2158	
2037		2067		2096		2127		2159	
2038		2068		2097		2128		2160	
2039		2069		2098		2129		2161	
2040		2070		2099		2130		2162	
2 Peter		2071		2100		2131		2163	
2041		2072		*Revelation*		2132		2164	
2042		2073		2101		2133		2165	
2043		2074		2102		2134		2166	
2044		2075		2103		2135		2167	
2045		2076		2104		2136		2168	
2046		2077		2105		2137		2169	
2047		2078		2106		2138		2170	
2048		2079		2107		2139		2171	
2049		2080		2108		2140		2172	
2050		2081		2109		2141		2173	
2051		*2 John*		2110		2142		2174	
1 John		2082		2111		2143		2175	
2052		2083		2112		2144		2176	
2053		2084		2113		2145		2177	
2054		2085		2114		2146		2178	

Question #	✔	Question #	✔	Question #	✔	Question #	✔	Question #	✔
2179		2211		2243		2275		2307	
2180		2212		2244		2276		2308	
2181		2213		2245		2277		2309	
2182		2214		2246		2278		2310	
2183		2215		2247		2279		2311	
2184		2216		2248		2280		2312	
2185		2217		2249		2281		2313	
2186		2218		2250		2282		2314	
2187		2219		2251		2283		2315	
2188		2220		2252		2284		2316	
2189		2221		2253		2285			
2190		2222		2254		2286			
2191		2223		2255		2287			
2192		2224		2256		2288			
2193		2225		2257		2289			
2194		2226		2258		2290			
2195		2227		2259		2291			
2196		2228		2260		2292			
2197		2229		2261		2293			
2198		2230		2262		2294			
2199		2231		2263		2295			
2200		2232		2264		2296			
2201		2233		2265		2297			
2202		2234		2266		2298			
2203		2235		2267		2299			
2204		2236		2268		2300			
2205		2237		2269		2301			
2206		2238		2270		2302			
2207		2239		2271		2303			
2208		2240		2272		2304			
2209		2241		2273		2305			
2210		2242		2274		2306			

Group Quiz Score Card

Here's 150 spaces for you to choose your own questions.
Make copies and set up a group challenge!

QUESTION #	CORRECT	INCORRECT	QUESTION #	CORRECT	INCORRECT	QUESTION #	CORRECT	INCORRECT	QUESTION #	CORRECT	INCORRECT	QUESTION #	CORRECT	INCORRECT

QUESTION #	CORRECT	INCORRECT	QUESTION #	CORRECT	INCORRECT	QUESTION #	CORRECT	INCORRECT	QUESTION #	CORRECT	INCORRECT	QUESTION #	CORRECT	INCORRECT

About the Author

Troy is a writer with credits in publishing, television, and video. Some of the highlights of his career include: the producer for the GSN game show *The American Bible Challenge*, writer of the popular Max Lucado series Hermie & Friends, host and writer of the GLO documentary *In His Shoes*, and writer for three seasons of *The Mickey Mouse Club*.

Troy is also a campus pastor at First Baptist Church of Windermere, Florida, where he has worked since 1997. He has written a number of books for children and inspirational books for adults.